Releasing Cancer Nature's Way:

True Healing
and How to Achieve It

True Healing Comes from Within

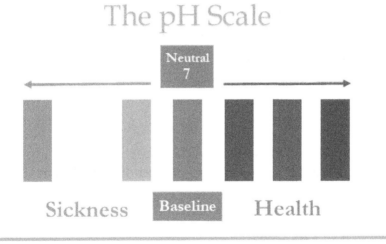

True Medicine Comes from the Earth

by Patricia Zimmerman

Releasing Cancer Nature's Way:

True Healing and How to Achieve It

Published and distributed in the United States by WDC Publishing. For information, contact WDC Publishing Co., Inc. at info.wdcpublishing@gmail.com.

Edited by Lisa Rose Schell
Proofread by Emma Grace Luckiw
Artist Rendering: Jessica Bledsoe

ISBN: 978-0-9962475-2-8
Library of Congress Cataloging-in-Publication Data: Not available at time of printing.

About the Author ...

Patricia M. Zimmerman is an ordained minister, spiritual counselor, metaphysical teacher, healing practitioner, published author, and founder of White Dove Circle of Light and Love, a spiritual, non-profit organization where one can find true healing for the mind, body, emotions, and spirit. She teaches classes on how to live life, looking at the self to bring about change. Her greatest teacher is life itself.

Dedication

This book is dedicated to my wonderful husband, Chuck, whom I love so very much! Thank you for all the love and support you have given me throughout our many years together so that I may walk this path and accomplish all my dreams, hopes, wishes, and desires. My love for you is eternal!

"The day science begins to study non-physical phenomena, it will make more progress in one decade than in all the previous centuries of its existence. To understand the true nature of the universe, one must think in terms of energy, frequency and vibration." — Nikola Tesla (1856 – 1943)

Acknowledgements

My sincerest and deepest gratitude to all those who have loved and supported me on my journey through life, for without you this book would not have been possible:

- To God—All There Is, Was, and Ever Shall Be, all of the High Angelic, Archangels, and Divine, to whom I dedicate my life and all that I do. Your unconditional love, wisdom, support, and guidance have helped me through times of confusion and turmoil. Your presence has been felt, guiding me every step of the way.

- To my parents whose unending love, support, faith, and principles have helped me to be the person I am today.

- To my husband, my children and their spouses, and to my grandchildren, whose unending love and respect have allowed my heart to open to an even deeper love than I have ever known.

- To Jim Wachter, Heather Kieffer, Peg Huneke, and Kay Brinkman, four people who have been with me since the founding of White Dove Circle of Light and Love in 2009. White Dove Circle wouldn't be where it is today without the love and support of these four beautiful souls. We have been through a lot together over the years and have helped each other learn many lessons along the way. It has been an incredible journey!

- To my dear friends, whose love and support has sustained me through my most challenging times in life, your input, guidance, and friendship will always be valued and treasured.

- To Jessica Bledsoe for her artistic talents that enable readers to "picture" the fourfold body, and to Emma Luckiw and Lisa Schell for taking the time to proof and edit this book.

Thank you, everyone, so very much. I love and appreciate you more than you will ever know!

Synopsis

Good health and well-being is something you pay for: You can pay for it now and enjoy healthy, delicious, and nutritious foods, or you can pay for it later in medical bills and an increased cost in health insurance. Until you look at your body as a long-term investment, you will not make the sacrifices necessary to attain the goal of good health.

Conventional medicine can be controlling, invasive, disabling, expensive, and dangerous. True medicine comes from the earth, not a lab. As Hippocrates once stated, "Let thy food be thy medicine and medicine be thy food."

True medicine is by far less expensive and can be easily found in fresh fruits and vegetables, especially leafy green vegetables. These natural foods include phytonutrients that nourish the body and antioxidants that regulate abnormal cell growth and stimulate apoptosis to regulate single cell death. ("Apo" means off. "Ptosis" means fall. Apoptosis is when a cell falls off or falls out. In other words, allowing the cell to be broken down and deliberately dismantled while adjacent cells remain unaffected.[1])

Prescription drugs mask symptoms. They do not heal. Symptoms can be released temporarily, but if the root cause of the dis-ease (energy not flowing with ease) is not released, it returns again in a similar or another form to show us what is going on within us.

At the root of all dis-ease is an emotion. The emotions behind cancer are anger and resentment. To truly heal, one must first release the emotions causing the overage of cancer in the body. Everyone has cancer in their body, but it is the overage of cancer that creates dis-ease within the physical body.

Once a person has a heartfelt desire to heal, there are three steps in healing: acceptance (accepting what happened), understanding

---

[1]

https://www.bing.com/videos/riverview/relatedvideo?&q=phytonutrients+that+nouris h+the+body+and+antioxidants+that+regulate+abnormal+cell+growth+and+stimulate +apoptosis+to+program+cell+death&qpvt=phytonutrients+that+nourish+the+body+a nd+antioxidants+that+regulate+abnormal+cell+growth+and+stimulate+apoptosis+to+ program+cell+death&mid=9A5AAC6852CDB08B4B2E9A5AAC6852CDB08B4B2 E&&FORM=VRDGAR

(understanding why/how it happened), and releasing (letting go; learning the lesson behind the dis-ease so it never returns). All true healing is releasing. It's that simple.

The information in this book can apply to all types of dis-ease held within the physical body, not just for cancer. It was written to let people know they hold the key to their own health and happiness, and once they come to understand how to properly care for their fourfold body (includes the mental, emotional, spiritual, and physical bodies), they will be amazed at how wonderful life can be.

Members of the medical establishment do have a role to play in our health. But too often medical practitioners treat the body not as a self-regulating and self-renewing wholistic organism but as a machine that breaks down.

There are many things the medical establishment can do that energy practitioners cannot, such as to perform surgery to repair damaged bodies, set broken bones, and help manage pain until the emotion causing the pain can be released. However, there are also many things energy practitioners can do that the medical establishment cannot. Both are needed.

Energy practitioners view their clients as whole—mental, emotional, spiritual, and physical. Our mental body is approximately ten percent of our being while our emotional body is approximately 90 percent of our being. This explains why the root of almost all dis-ease goes back to an emotion. The key to true healing is to find the root cause (trauma) causing the emotion and work to release it.

While I am not a medical doctor and have no formal training in medicine, I have witnessed what medical personnel would call "miracles," but which I know to be simply "healing from the inside out" the way the body was designed to work. I am a teacher, energy practitioner, and spiritual counselor. My focus is on healing the mind, emotions, and spirit. Once the mind, emotions, and spirit have been healed, the physical body will heal itself. This I know to be true for I have personally witnessed it take place many, many times over the past thirty plus years that I have been practicing energy healing. Anything and everything is possible if we just believe.

Are you ready to heal? Better yet, are you ready to look at yourself? If you are ready for true healing, this book is for you. Empower yourself! The time for change is now, and it all begins with YOU!

Table of Contents

Introduction

Even when it seems dark, there is always light. Even when you feel there is no hope, there is love. Even when you think you can't go on, there is God! You are God and God is you! Keep your faith in self, in light and love, and you will see that all will be well. ~ All There Is, Was, and Ever Shall Be through Elliott Eli Jackson[2]

Cancer ... the very sound of this word evokes fear in the minds of men and women. People who hear they have cancer live in fear, the fear they will die from it one day. But they do not have to die from cancer. They can live. People release cancer all the time, and they continue to live life.

Having a purpose in life is important. Without a sense of purpose and a proper perspective on life, life can become hopeless. We begin to fear death. FEAR (False Evidence Appearing Real) is the most destructive energy in the universe. Instead, we should be living life with joy and excitement, being in service to one another.

Fear is the absence of love. Where fear exists, love cannot. Once a person goes into fear, they can't stop thinking negatively about what will happen to them. They focus on the negative instead of the positive. The more we focus on something, the more we create it. You are a creator! Always focus on what you want more of in life, never what you don't want.

Everyone has cancer in their physical body. It is the overage of cancer that creates illness or dis-ease (energy not flowing with ease) in the body. Cancer is not the problem. The overage of cancer in the body is the problem.

Too much or too little of anything in life can create problems. Let's take water, for example. Too much water creates a flood; too little water creates a drought. Water is not the problem. It is the amount of

---

water that creates the problem. Similarly, if you put too much or too little oil in your car, it will break down. The same will happen with your body.

The human body is a finely tuned, well designed instrument. An excess amount or depletion of any vitamin, supplement, mineral, amino acid, etc. can throw the body out of balance. Moderation and balance, within and without, are the keys to living life with ease and grace.

The same holds true for cancer. So, what causes an overage of cancer in the body? Is it something in our food (preservatives, food coloring, processed sugar, etc.)? Is it something in our environment (chemicals, chemtrails, etc.)? Is it emotional (anger and resentment)? Or is it karmic (something to be balanced/resolved from the past or from a past life)?

And why is it that people who are physically fit get cancer? Why are some cancers fast-growing and others slow growing? Why do some people die from cancer and some live? Is cancer hereditary, or is it a learned behavior? So many questions, so many possibilities.

Is there a cure for cancer? Many people believe the medical establishment has a cure but will not make it available because there are no profits to be made without patients. It is more profitable to "maintain" an illness rather than to cure an illness. Most studies are sponsored by pharmaceutical companies that are producing the drugs and the treatments, adding to already-biased conclusions compared with independent studies not sponsored by these companies.[3]

Do cancer therapies really work? This is debatable. Numbers are often manipulated in studies to create the desired outcome. It is important to understand how statistics are derived because we are all different. Each of us comes from a different background, and each person handles life differently. We have different body and skin types; ethnic, religious, and cultural backgrounds; eating habits and behavior patterns; etc. How does all this information play into recorded statistics? Humanity is diverse. We are not a "one size fits all" society.

---

[3] https://www.youtube.com/watch?v=JSV4VZ8gdUQ, *Trust in Research—the ethics of knowledge production,* Garry Gray, *TedXVictoria*

Once cancer can no longer be measured in the body, patients are told their cancer has gone into "remission," meaning it can come back again in a similar or different part of the body. In other words, it has not been completely released.

Join me on a journey to better understand how to release cancer naturally, without drugs, surgery, or radiation. Learn what true healing is and how to achieve it. The principles in this book can be applied to any dis-ease, not just cancer. If the principles are followed, the body can and will heal, and life can and will get better because synchronicity takes place when you are in the flow of life. You will be living life from a place of love. The only thing that stops us in life is fear.

Someone I personally know once said to me, "And what degree do you have that makes you so smart?" To which I replied, "Common sense!" And a good understanding of the fourfold body, something doctors and research scientists know little about.

In order to understand what true healing is and how to achieve it, one must fully understand the mind, body, emotion, and spirit connection. They must be able to determine the "root" of the dis-ease and work to release it. The root is never in the physical body.

We are fourfold beings. Only one of our bodies is physical. If you only look at the physical body for answers, you are missing the bigger picture. To find the root, one must go within.

Everything begins with a thought. If a belief is attached to the thought, we add emotion to the thought. The more emotion we add to the belief, the faster we create the outcome. This is how we create our world. Thoughts are things, and they are held in the mental body. Emotion is stored in the emotional body.

Our spirit body is identical to our physical body and resides within it. Most pain is held within the spirit body, not the physical body. Because we view ourselves as humans having a spiritual experience, we believe pain is held in the physical body. This is not true. Your physical body is the vehicle which your spirit chose to maneuver around earth.

If you are in an accident while driving your car, who feels the pain? Your car does not, but you do. Your car may get damaged, but it does not feel pain. Your spirit feels pain because emotion is present. We are spirits having a human experience.

When we die, we shed the physical body. The mental, emotional, and spirit bodies stay intact and incarnate into another body, similar to a snake shedding its skin, for the spirit never dies. When we see a corpse, we immediately know the spirit has left the body because it is the spirit that moves the physical body. In other words, the spirit no longer resides within the physical body.

For true and lasting healing to take place, the mental, emotional, and spirit bodies must be healed and balanced. The physical body will automatically adapt once these three important bodies have healed because the physical body reflects what is taking place within.

Keep an open mind while reading this book. Much of the experience of life is lost when a person is close-minded. Life is filled with truths and non-truths. It is up to us to discern which is truth and which is not. One can only go as far as their depth of understanding and comprehension will allow.

The higher you raise your vibration, the more you can see and understand truth. In other words, you can't make a kindergartner do college-level work. A kindergartener will never be able to understand quantum physics. He or she must build a foundation of knowledge to be able to better understand something more complex.

Science and spirituality are one and can never be separated. Life can be simple (spirituality), yet complex (scientifically). Learn to get out of your own way. You are the master of your own life and destiny.

Create Beauty ~ Love Yourself, Love Others ~ Live Life, Love Life

The Choice is Always YOURS!

There Is Reason and Purpose for Everything

The medical establishment manages physical symptoms, working from the outside in. True healing takes place from the inside out. The mind, body, emotions, and spirit must be balanced for true healing to take place. Until the majority of the medical establishment recognizes the role the mind, emotions, and spirit play in our health, their understanding will be limited as to how the physical body really heals.
~ Patricia M. Zimmerman[4]

There is reason and purpose for everything in life, including cancer. Cancer, considered a hereditary dis-ease by the medical establishment, may run in a family, but the type of cancer is not always the same for the afflicted person. I cannot prove dis-ease is hereditary. This idea implies limited thinking and victimhood. There are no victims in life! We had a choice in every situation on some level, especially if it is the result of karma.

Cancer eats away at the physical body, and repressed anger "eats" away at the emotional body. There are hundreds of different types of cancer, and there are hundreds of different emotions that eat away at us. Where the cancer lands in the body is determined by the emotion experienced.

The brain, your computer, connects to your mental body (the mind). The remainder of your physical body connects to your emotional body. Problems with the brain represent a negative way of thinking. Problems with the rest of the body represent a negative way of feeling. Each body part stores a different emotion. A "common sense" list of body parts, symptoms, and dis-eases and what they represent can be found in the Appendix of this book. Take time to listen to your body. What is it trying to tell you? Listen to the words of others. They are often your

---

4 *Self-Empowerment: The Only Way to Heal* by Patricia Zimmerman © 2012 by WDC Publishing Co., Inc. All rights reserved.

words. When you change your way of thinking, the change will be reflected in your body.

A good example of how healing works is that of a cookie in a cookie jar. Unless you connect with the cookie (an emotion), you will never get it out of the cookie jar (the emotional body). True and permanent healing takes place as we release the "cookies" (emotions from past and present lives) stored within.

Physical Issues and Diseases

The following excerpt is from the book, *The Sapiential Discourses: Universal Wisdom, Book 3*, pages 169-171, by All There Is, Was, and Ever Shall Be through Elliott Eli Jackson:

"Keep in mind that what WE will discuss now also is relative to issues of the physical, such as heart issues, weight gain, weight loss, and other issues that affect that portion of the fourfold being. This is to further state or inform you that you plan, from the beginning, includes what the optimal weight should be for your body frame at any given point in your life. However, the dietary and supplemental intake of your encasement plays a major role here. If you have come to a high level of vibration which would be guided by the spiritual portion of your being, one will be at, what you may call, a healthy weight for its encasement. If your vibration, spiritually, is not as high as it should be, over or undereating may occur. This, of course, will affect your weight.

"Now because the nature of lower vibrational portions of US is to cause one not to like self, WE will use this term, one can be influenced to do certain things. For instance—to not curtail eating habits, to eat large portions of meat, or to under eat and, of course, not to take the appropriate vitamins and supplemental intake for oneself. However, once again, in the Soul Plan, the optimal weight has been set.

"What should and does happen if and when one obtains the truthful information about self, that you are beautiful and wonderful, is to cause your plan to take its full scope and potential. Thus, the exercise, eating, and supplemental intake will be appropriate for your being. Then the weight loss or gain, whichever is necessary, will happen or occur.

22

"Let US now look at the acquisition of dis-eases. WE will be using or explaining this as it relates to cancer. Within the Soul Plan of many is the taking on of a measure of cancer that is over what is set for the human body on your planet within the Gadius Universal Plan. Remember, all of you have everything within your being, this includes cancer. However, it is in the set trace amount. Now within the Plan of a soul or spirit could be the acquisition of an overage of such. If there is within the Plan, it would be for one of the following purposes:

- **The acceptance of disease, by the person, which will cause the being to push the cancer out, heal oftentimes without any logical explanation, and assist others in doing the same in the future.**
- **Acquire such, accept, and not to push the cancer away. The reason or purpose for this would be to assist others with acceptance, compassion, and other feelings and emotions connected to their concept of death on planet Earth. If this is the case, then the purpose of the overage of cancer is and was to help your others deal with, once again, themselves and their views on and about acceptance and death.**
- **To acquire such and attached to it the message or gift of assisting others in understanding that control is an illusion, and that each soul has its own path.** *Fore, the death, as you call it, will be what you may term as a graceful one. This would mean, there will be no external complaining about the carrier's plight in life or why they obtained the disease.*
- **To acquire such, push it away and allow it to come back once, twice, or many times. If this is the case, it has to do with the mental of the encasement accepting some kind of truth connected to consistence in maintaining proper care of self in all four areas of the human being— spiritual, mental, emotional, and physical.**

  If this understanding is obtained, the cancer will leave and not return. If not accepted, the cancer will result in

what you term as death and the carrier will return in another encasement later to experience the same.

"The above scenarios will be the case concerning all major diseases, as you understand the term, that are considered possible on your home, your planet, your Earth, to be life threatening. **Further, be it known that attached to each disease that may be in one's plan are gifts for understanding. These gifts are designed to assist one or more of you on its soul's or spirit's personal journey.** Set within the Soul Plan, attached to the acquiring of disease, is the ability to consciously use the disease as an opportunity to bring about spiritual growth and the uplifting of one's vibrational level. All Soul Plans are constructed to assist one in the understanding that everything and everyone that comes into one's life are presented to give and receive gifts. And, yes, WE do mean **EVERYTHING!** All is for motivation, and fine tuning of other emotions, which includes **Love.**

"Additionally, all is designed to push one toward acceptance of self and others. Now, there is no need for forgiveness of self and others during a lifetime, fore, none of you have ever done anything wrong. You have only done that which you could do with the information given to you connected to the vibrational level that you were or are at. You can act no other way until you accept other information and/or raise your vibration. This is what "It is what it is" really means. **Yet there is always room for the acceptance and understanding of what you have created in your life.** This means you take responsibility for what you created in your life. Fore, what you created through your actions, reactions, and behaviors in dealing with self and others, affects your personal Soul Plan. **Remember,** all is connected, even if you wish it were not. Therefore, the acceptance of such allows the blueprint of your life to flow as it should, or begin to flow as it was designed to, whatever the case may be. All in the Soul Plan is set to lead to one and only one unavoidable eventuality."

Healing: A Spiritual Perspective

Do not believe in what you have heard; do not believe in traditions because they have been handed down for many generations; do not believe anything because it is rumored and spoken of by many; do not believe merely because the written instruments of some old sage are produced; do not believe in conjectures; do not believe in that as a truth to which you have become attached by habit; do not believe merely on the authority of your teachers and elders. After observation and analysis, when it agrees with reason and is conducive to the good and benefit of one and all, then accept it and live up to it. – Gautama Buddha

Never use the word "survivor" as it implies you were a victim in life. There are no victims in life, only co-creators of circumstances. It is more fitting to use the word "champion" than it is survivor.

The only one who heals is the person him or herself, when he or she is ready. Poor health and dis-ease do not "just happen." When a person can accept responsibility for the mistakes of the past, then it is time to move into a new way of thinking and begin to reverse the dis-ease process.

Research scientists and doctors look to the physical body for answers. Rarely do they look at what is taking place emotionally in a patient's life.

At the root of every dis-ease is an emotion. At the root of every dis-ease is a life lesson. If the lesson has not been learned, and if the behavior has not been changed permanently, the dis-ease will return when similar emotions are experienced.

Sometimes dis-ease is a way to leave the body. We chose an exit plan before we came into this incarnation. If the onset of dis-ease was fast (such as cancer or a heart attack) and death was quick, most likely it was a way that person chose to leave the earth plane. If a person lingered awhile before dying, he or she may have been burning off karma before leaving, or had unfinished business to take care of, or may have been given an opportunity to finish something and forgive. Everything happens for a reason and a purpose.

We choose the manner in which we experience dis-ease and the manner in which we heal. We choose what we will accept and what we won't, what we will believe and what we won't. When fear enters the picture, it holds us captive. We become paralyzed. Fear is the only thing that stops us from moving forward in life. It can also take our life.

True healing cannot begin until you accept responsibility for your role in the situation. No one can or will do it for you.

Take a step back and be the observer. Look at the situation from a different perspective. Look at the whole picture, not just what you want to see. What was your role in creating the situation? What lessons were you learning?

You cannot change anyone else. In order for your life to change, you must be the one to change. And when you shift your way of thinking and begin to see things differently, your world will change with you.

The Hand in the Glove

Picture in your mind a hand with a glove over it. The hand represents our spirit body and the glove represents our physical body. Without the hand, the glove cannot move. We see the glove, but we don't always see the spirit moving the glove.

When there is blood on the glove, where do you think the blood came from? The hand inside the glove; in other words, the spirit inside the physical body.

When doctors see blood on the glove (physical body), they clean it up and bandage the wound. When I see blood on the glove, I see someone whose joy is leaving, for blood represents the joy in life. In order to heal, that person must find joy in their life once more.

When a doctor sees a lump on the glove, he or she will probably want to remove it. When I look at the lump, I see someone who is nursing old hurts and building remorse. In order to heal, that person must learn forgiveness.

Doctors only treat the physical body. Energy practitioners treat the spirit body. All dis-ease begins with an emotion. Even stress is an emotion. When the spirit body heals, the physical body will also heal. This is what is known as "self" healing.

Dis-ease begins in the spirit body and flows into the physical body when the spirit body can hold no more. Dis-ease in the physical body is a way to get our attention to show us what is going on within us.

The cut, burn, and poison methods used to treat cancer kill the spirit long before it kills the dis-ease in the physical body. It's time we begin looking to the spirit to heal the physical body.

You Have a Right to Know!

You have a right to answers from the medical establishment. Doctors are not gods, even though we sometimes treat them as if they are.

Protect yourself by asking your physician questions about the care you are being given and the pills being prescribed. Get a second opinion. Gather information from credible sources. The Internet is a good source to find answers. Many major hospitals have information on illnesses on their website.

Bring all of your prescription drugs to your doctor when you visit so he knows exactly what you are taking. Pharmacies have been known to fill a prescription with the wrong drug, sometimes resulting in death.

A good book tailored to physicians, nurses, pharmacists, physician assistants, and consumers containing information on brand names, adult and pediatric dosages, how to use, warnings and precautions, adverse reactions, drug interactions, storage, and more is the *Physicians Desk Reference* (PDR).

A good website to find information on clinical trials is PubMed. This website comprises more than 24 million citations for biomedical literature from MEDLINE, life science journals, and online books.

When looking at websites, be careful to watch who is sponsoring the website. If it is a pharmaceutical company, search for another website.

Here are some questions to ask your doctor about dis-eases and prescription pills:

Dis-eases
- Where can I find more information on the topic and its current research status?
- Are there alternative, natural methods to treat this illness? If so, what are they?

Prescription Drugs
- Has this drug been approved for this symptom or illness, or has it been approved for a different symptom or illness? Where do you get your information?
- If it has been approved for your illness, how many test subjects were given this drug under scientific conditions? Where do you get your information?
- How much more effective is this drug than a placebo? Where do you get your information?
- What are the side effects of the pill? What are the side effects of the pill when taken with other pills? Where do you get your information?

Always ask your doctor if he would take the drug him or herself. Then ask your doctor if he or she would let his children and grandchildren take the drug.

God gave us everything to sustain life in a plant whether it is the food we eat or the remedy we take when we don't feel good. If God made it, trust it. If man made it, question it. God knows best.

Don't be afraid to try integrated healing *before* you see the doctor. It is cost-effective, non-invasive, and really works! Once you put a name to your dis-ease, you own it. It becomes much harder to release.

Stand in Your Power

The more we feed a fear, the more power it has over us. There is nothing more destructive than fear. And that includes the fear we face when we get sick.

During a Hospice training workshop I once attended, a movie was shown that included a woman talking about how she had feared for a long time that she would get cancer, and then she did. She talked about how she feared ending up in a wheelchair as a result of the cancer, and then she did. Her fear was so strong that she drew the dis-ease and the disability to her. This woman *believed* she was going to get both, and she did.

There are different ways to treat dis-ease. What may work for one person may not work for you. Side effects that happened to others do not have to happen to you. And when energy work is involved in your healing, the results are much better—healing comes much faster and with fewer, if any, side effects.

The medical profession is trained to treat the masses, not the individual. If a doctor tells you what to expect with the dis-ease, that information is based on other peoples' experiences. They are not your experiences. If you believe you will get a disease and its side effects, you will. If you believe you won't, you won't. Energy follows attention. The more you believe something will happen, the more you create it or draw it to you.

Since science has proven everything is energy. why not heal energy with energy? To fix a crack in the ceiling, we do not tape, then paint over it. The crack will be masked; it will still be there. But if you take the same component that the wall is made of and use it to fill in the crack, then smooth and paint over it, you will never know the crack was ever there. Energy healing is an effective tool for healing.

Money is power (purchasing power). Don't blindly accept what your doctor tells you as truth. Do your research. Contrary to popular belief, doctors do not have all the answers. The more money we spend on doctor visits, medications, health insurance, etc. and the more we talk about our health problems and the pills we take; the more we "buy" into a particular way of "being." We become "invested" in our illness. What are you "buying" into? Is your long-term health worth the price?

Knowledge is power. Question, question, question everything. It is your right, and it will empower you. Use discernment to know what is best for you. Know all your options. Become informed. Get a second and a third opinion, if necessary. Use common sense, and then use your purchasing power in a way that best benefits you and your loved ones.

Truth is power. What we have been taught—and what we believe—is not always the truth. Research scientists change their truth daily based on new research findings. One month we should not eat butter; the next month, butter is fine. One year, eggs can kill us; the next year, they are part of a healthy diet. Our perception of truth is constantly changing, based on our experiences and what we have learned. New things are learned every day.

Know what is best for *you*! Know yourself well enough to know what will work and what will not work. You are unique and individual. There is no one else just like you. Have the courage to do what is right for you, not what is right for someone else. How you handle a dis-ease is your responsibility. Don't give your power away to others by letting them make decisions for you. For you deserve the very best life has to offer!

Cancer

The more we fear cancer, the more we believe we will get it, the more we draw it to us. The lesson to be learned is one of faith. A strong faith can overcome any fear. It is possible to move mountains—the mountains we make out of molehills in life. ~ Patricia M. Zimmerman[5]

From a spiritual perspective, all dis-ease comes from a negative emotion. Cancer eats away at a body no different than a negative emotion can eat away at a person. The more we repress an emotion internally, the more it will eat away at us until eventually, the emotion overflows into the physical body as dis-ease.

The root emotions of cancer are anger and resentment. Each body part holds a different type of emotion. For example, the kidneys hold feelings of being "pissed off." Joy in life is stored in the blood. Reproductive organs store lessons not learned. Victimhood is stored in the pancreas. (See Appendix, "Body Parts and Symptoms: What They Represent Spiritually")

From a medical perspective, cancer begins when old or abnormal cells don't die when they should. As cancer cells grow out of control, they crowd out normal cells. This makes it hard for your body to work the way it was designed.[6]

What is Cancer?

Cancer, the second leading cause of death in the world, is a complex disease that occurs when abnormal cells in the body grow and divide uncontrollably, forming a growth or tumor. These cancer cells invade and destroy the tissue around them. A tumor has metastasized when it breaks away from the organs on which they are growing and travel to other parts of the body, where they continue to grow. The

---

[5] *Self-Empowerment: The Only Way to Heal* by Patricia Zimmerman © 2012 by WDC Publishing Co., Inc. All rights reserved.
[6] https://www.cancer.org/cancer/understanding-cancer/what-is-cancer.html

cancer cells eventually travel throughout the body by invading the two systems that feed all of the body's organs: the bloodstream and lymph system.[7]

A whole-body PET/CT scan can help physicians effectively pinpoint the source of cancer to determine whether or not the cancer is isolated to one specific area or if it has spread to other organs.

The History of Cancer

Cancer has been around throughout recorded history dating back to ancient Egypt. Some of the earliest evidence has been found in decomposed bones, mummies, and ancient manuscripts.

The Greek physician Hippocrates (460-370 BC) used the terms *carcinos* and *carcinoma* to describe non-ulcer forming and ulcer-forming tumors. In Greek, these words refer to a crab, most likely because the finger-like spreading projections of a cancer are often in the shape of a crab. The Roman physician, Celsus (25 BC - 50 AD), later translated the Greek term into *cancer*, the Latin word for crab. Galen (130-200 AD), another Greek physician, used the word *oncos* (Greek for swelling) to describe tumors. Although the crab analogy of Hippocrates and Celsus is still used to describe malignant tumors, Galen's term is used today as a part of the name for cancer specialists (oncologists).

In 1761, Giovanni Morgagni of Padua performed autopsies to understand the patient's illness to pathologic findings after death. This laid the foundation for scientific oncology, the study of cancer.

The Scottish surgeon John Hunter (1728-1793) suggested some cancers might be cured by surgery and taught how surgeons might decide which cancers to operate on. If the tumor had not invaded nearby tissue and was "moveable," he said, "There is no impropriety in removing it."

Anesthesia allowed surgery to prosper. Cancer operations, such as the radical mastectomy, developed as a result.

---

[7] https://www.mayoclinic.org/diseases-conditions/cancer/symptoms-causes/syc-20370588

Scientific oncology began using microscopes to study diseased tissues during the 19th century. Rudolf Virchow, the founder of cellular pathology, provided the scientific basis for the modern pathologic study of cancer. Morgagni linked autopsy findings seen with the unaided eye with the clinical course of illness, while Virchow correlated microscopic pathology to illness, allowing a better understanding how cancer can progress. A precise diagnosis could be made upon examination of body tissues removed by a surgeon. The pathologist could also tell the surgeon whether the operation had completely removed the cancer.[8]

Cancer Has Become an Epidemic

Cancer has become an epidemic as a result of "awareness." Just hearing the word "cancer" can evoke fear in a person. The color pink used to represent love, but today when people think of pink, they think of breast cancer. And this fear comes wrapped in a "ribbon" to make it look pretty.

Several studies have forecasted an increase in breast cancer in the upcoming decades. A study done in 2015 and led by Philip Rosenberg, Ph.D., of NCI's Division of Cancer Epidemiology and Genetics, confirmed "the forecasted increase in U.S. breast cancer cases diagnosed each year, concluding that they will grow from 283,000 cases in 2011 to 441,000 in 2030—a more than 50 percent increase." [9] Breast cancer is only one of over 150 types of cancer.

According to the American Cancer Society, "In 2022, approximately 20 million cancer cases were newly diagnosed and 9.7 million people died from the disease worldwide. By 2050, the number of cancer cases is predicted to increase to 35 million based solely on projected population growth." [10]

---

[8] https://www.cancer.org/cancer/understanding-cancer/history-of-cancer/what-is-cancer.html

[9] https://www.cancer.gov/news-events/cancer-currents-blog/2015/breast-forecast

[10] https://www.cancer.org/research/cancer-facts-statistics/global-cancer-facts-and-figures.html

Pharmaceutical companies are aware of how dependent we have become on pills. They use subliminal messages to sell their products. Instead of getting healthier, we are collectively becoming sicker as time goes on.

Why is the number of cancer patients steadily increasing instead of decreasing over time? Clearly, health is not something money can buy. If it were, citizens of the United States would be the healthiest in the world.

From what I have seen, the answer is partly because of fear. The more we fear something, the more we draw it to us. The more reminders there are around us, the more seeds are planted to help us connect with fear and create dis-ease. We so fear the disease that we have invented more and more methods of detecting it, even those cancers that will never interfere with the person's health.

Symptoms of Cancer

Signs and symptoms caused by cancer vary depending on the afflicted body part. Following are some general signs and symptoms associated with, but not specific to, cancer:
- Fatigue
- Lump or area of thickening that can be felt under the skin
- Weight changes, including unintended loss or gain
- Skin changes, such as yellowing, darkening or redness of the skin, sores that won't heal, or changes to existing moles
- Changes in bowel or bladder habits
- Persistent cough or trouble breathing
- Difficulty swallowing
- Hoarseness
- Persistent indigestion or discomfort after eating
- Persistent, unexplained muscle or joint pain
- Persistent, unexplained fevers or night sweats
- Unexplained bleeding or bruising

If you have any persistent signs or symptoms that concern you, be sure to consult your doctor. [11]

Cancer is a Booming Industry

Americans spend an unbelievable amount of money every year in a search for "cures" for everything from heart disease to cancer to depression. Cancer alone is a multi-billion-dollar business. Over the past decade, sales revenues from cancer drugs among top pharmaceutical companies have increased by nearly 100 percent, from $52.8 billion in 2010 to $103.5 billion in 2019. [12]

The Center for Disease Control and Prevention (CDC) reported in 2019, "the national patient economic burden associated with cancer care was estimated to be $21.09 billion. This estimate includes patient out-of-pocket costs of over $16 billion and patient time costs of over $5 billion." It stated these findings are important because the high cost of cancer treatment paid by insurers, out-of-pocket expenses, and patient time make cancer a health priority. [13]

Out-of-pocket expenses for health care include a person's share of prescription drugs and medical services, provider and outpatient visits, emergency room visits, and hospital inpatient stays not covered by insurance, as well as copays, deductibles, and coinsurance. Someone who doesn't have health insurance or with limited coverage may be responsible for the entire cost of care.

Following are some key facts and figures on the cost of cancer from the Cancer Action Network™ of the American Cancer Society:

---

[11] https://www.mayoclinic.org/diseases-conditions/cancer/symptoms-causes/syc-20370588

[12] https://dailynews.ascopubs.org/do/sales-revenue-cancer-drugs-has-doubled-among-top-pharmaceutical-companies-last-10-years

[13] https://blogs.cdc.gov/cancer/2021/10/26/the-cost-of-cancer/#:~:text=In%202019%2C%20the%20national%20patient%20economic%20burden%20associated,age%2C%20stage%20at%20diagnosis%2C%20and%20phase%20of%20care.

Patient Costs
- A 2019 report in the Journal of American Medicine found that 44 percent of cancer patients deplete their life savings and 62 percent go into debt.
- One in three cancer survivors reported "job lock" for their household because of their cancer diagnosis according to a JAMA Oncology study. In 2015, Americans lost $94 billion in earnings because of a cancer diagnosis. Job lock refers to a circumstance in which a worker would like to retire or stop working altogether but perceives they cannot due to a need for income and/or health insurance to exist.[14]

Prescription Costs
- Patients are more likely to let prescriptions go unfilled when they face out-of pocket costs. According to a recent study in the Journal of Clinical Oncology, one-third of patients abandoned prescriptions when facing high out-of pocket cost.[15]
- The National Cancer Institute estimates that a patient's out-of-pocket costs can be up to $12,000 per year for certain drugs.

Stress and Anxiety
- An American Cancer Society Cancer Action Network (ACS CAN) survey conducted in 2018 found that 51 percent of patients reported struggles with anxiety or depression.[16]
- A majority of cancer patients want to talk to their doctor about costs, but only 27 percent of patients and less than half of oncologists report having had a discussion about cost according to a survey from the National Cancer Institute.[17]

[14] https://www.ncbi.nlm.nih.gov/pmc/articles/PMC6711468/
[15] https://pubmed.ncbi.nlm.nih.gov/29261440/
[16]
https://www.fightcancer.org/sites/default/files/docs/2020%20Cost%20of%20Cancer%20Facts%20&%20Figures.pdf
[17]
https://www.fightcancer.org/sites/default/files/docs/2020%20Cost%20of%20Cancer%20Facts%20&%20Figures.pdf

Wouldn't it be nice if this money was spent on more enjoyable ways to stay healthy, like vacations, continuing education, hobbies, family activities, and more?

Cancer is a growing business. Have you noticed how many large buildings today belong to hospitals, cancer treatment centers, rehab centers, outpatient clinics, pharmacies, and other "care" centers? Have you noticed the amount money spent on marketing and advertising, not just for pharmaceuticals, but for health care institutions as well? Have you noticed the number of buildings carrying the name of a major hospital or health care provider? How about the number of billboards, signs on buses, and even advertisements that come right to your door via the mail?

There are constant reminders of dis-ease everywhere you turn. Seeds are being planted, and those seeds use fear, a very powerful subliminal tool, as its base. Not only are we bombarded with constant reminders of dis-ease, businesses everywhere hope to profit from it. Even banks benefit from the advertising of a dis-ease ("open an account with us").

Consider the amount of money spent:

- to support the administration of various health care institutions (e.g., hospitals, rehab centers, clinical laboratories, research facilities, treatment centers, pharmacies, insurance companies, medical equipment and supplies, computer systems, advertising, printing, etc.) that support cancer awareness and treatment.
- on schooling to become a health care professional. A medical education is very expensive. Banks make money on college loans.
- on the different procedures and cancer therapies (e.g., chemo-therapy, surgery, radiation, etc.).

Do you see where this is going? How many people and industries are supported each year by cancer alone, let alone other dis-eases? The number is immense and incredible. We have become a sick society.

What if a cure for cancer were to be found? How many people would lose their jobs? What would they do for a living? How would our lives change?

So the question now is, does the medical establishment really want people to heal? Better yet, do we really want to heal?

Researchers in the field of medical science are constantly expanding their knowledge, searching for new and improved understandings of the human body and for different and better ways to heal it. Yet after all these years they still do not fully understand why some people get sick and others do not, why some people heal and others do not—and they never will until they begin to look beyond the physical body itself. We, as humans, are more than simply physical bodies. We are spirits having a human experience.

As long as a person is getting something out of their illness, they will not heal. There are trade-offs with everything in life. Sometimes people hang onto an illness because the fear of dealing with a situation is worse than the pain of the illness itself. Believe it or not, some people use their illness to get attention or because they do not want to work. Other people have had their illness so long they have "become" their illness. They have lost sight of who they really were before they got sick. In other words, it has become their identity. And sometimes illness is karmic. For instance, someone who has lost the use of his or her legs may have to learn to stand up for him or herself. There are many reasons we hang onto illness.

What would we do or talk about if we weren't sick or know someone who was sick? Life would definitely be different if there were less illness. It would be much better. We would be able to enjoy life and all it has to offer. We would thrive, not just survive.

People begin to get better when they become sick and tired of being sick and tired. As long as there is a patient to care for, the health care industry and all those associated with it will continue to remain big business.

Conventional Cancer Treatments

A good doctor is a patient advocate, not a sickness care advocate. There is a difference. Our current medical system is not a true health care system. It is a "sickness" care system.

We have become a pill-popping society. Not only is there a name for every malady, there is a pill to help manage it. If a doctor were to put you on a plant-based diet and you got better, he or she probably wouldn't see you again.

Many people find it easier to take a pill than to change an eating habit or make a lifestyle change. Doctors find it easier to prescribe a pill than to lose a patient. Ultimately, we are responsible for our own health, and sooner or later, if we are not careful, the number of pills we take each day and the cost of these pills will catch up to us.

Following are basic information on the different conventional cancer treatments available today, as well as their side effects.

Chemotherapy

Chemotherapy began in the 1940's. It involves taking different forms of drugs, such as antitumor, antibiotics that prevent cancer cells from copying their DNA, and antimetabolites which prevent cancer cells from creating genetic material needed to create new cells, just to name a few.[18]

However, while these drugs can kill off cancer, they are poison to the body because they cannot tell the difference between fast-growing cancer cells and other fast-growing cells, such as blood, skin, and stomach cells. This is why many individuals undergoing chemotherapy experience unpleasant side effects.[19]

The goal is to prevent cancer cells from dividing and multiplying. Success and survival rates vary from person to person. Cancer stages indicate how large a tumor is and how far its cells have spread throughout the body.[20]

Chemotherapy can be given in different ways: infusions, pills, shots, creams, drugs, and wafers. How often a treatment is received is determined by the drug(s) taken and how well the body recovers after each treatment. Treatments can be continuous or there may be a break between treatments.

---

[18] https://my.clevelandclinic.org/health/treatments/24323-chemotherapy-drugs
[19] https://www.nhsinform.scot/tests-and-treatments/non-surgical-procedures/chemotherapy#:~:text=Even%20though%20chemotherapy
[20] https://www.medicalnewstoday.com/articles/326031

While each drug has its own side effects, common side effects of chemotherapy include: nausea, vomiting, diarrhea, hair loss, loss of appetite, fatigue, fever, mouth sores, pain, constipation, easy bruising, and bleeding.[21]

Long-lasting side effects can include: bone conditions, heart conditions, kidney conditions, and lung conditions, early menopause, cognitive problems, mental health conditions, hair and hearing loss, fatigue, endocrine symptoms, infertility, nerve damage, dental issues, memory issues, osteoporosis, problems with digestion, and increased risk of other cancers.[22]

Chemotherapy affects each person differently. Some effects occur during treatment while other effects may not show up until months or years after treatment. Some complications may be permanent, while others may disappear over time. [23]

Chemotherapy goes into the bloodstream and travels through every part of the body, not just the afflicted part. According to the Dana-Farber Cancer Institute, some drugs leave the body in a few days, while others may take up to seven days to be cleared.[24] Unfortunately, no research has been done to date to show how long these drugs stay in the body.

Radiation

Radiation began at the beginning of the twentieth century. Radiation incorporates beams of intense energy to kill cancer cells. It can be given inside or outside the body. Radiation damages cells by destroying their genetic material (how cells grow and divide). In the process, healthy cells may also be damaged along with the damaged cells. Radiation can also be used to shrink tumors and stop the growth of remaining cancer cells. According to the Mayo Clinic, more than

[21] https://www.mayoclinic.org/tests-procedures/chemotherapy/about/pac-20385033

[22] https://www.mayoclinic.org/diseases-conditions/cancer/in-depth/cancer-survivor/art-20045524

[23] https://www.medicalnewstoday.com/articles/long-term-side-effects-of-chemotherapy#long-term-effects

[24] https://blog.dana-farber.org/insight/2022/06/how-long-does-chemotherapy-stay-in-your-body/

half of all people with cancer will receive radiation therapy as part of their treatment.[25]

Side effects of radiation include: hair loss, skin irritation, fatigue, nausea, vomiting, diarrhea, early menopause, infertility, heart and vascular problems, risk of stroke, lung disease, lymphedema, hypothyroidism, osteoporosis, dry mouth, thickened saliva, difficulty swallowing, sore throat, changes in the way food tastes, mouth sores, cavities and tooth decay, intestinal problems, bladder irritation, frequent urination, memory issues, sexual dysfunction, and increased risk of other cancers. Side effects can be developed after treatment.[26]

Cancer Surgery

Cancer surgery is often used in conjunction with other cancer treatments such as chemotherapy and radiation. It involves cutting out the cancer, as well as some healthy tissue around it. Lymph nodes may also be removed if they contain cancer cells. If cancer spreads to the lymph nodes, there is a high probability it will travel to other parts of the body.

Typical cancer surgery techniques include: cryosurgery, electrosurgery, laser surgery, Mohs surgery, laparoscopic surgery, robotic surgery, and natural orifice surgery.

Side effects of cancer surgery include: pain, infection, loss of organ function, fatigue, bleeding, blood clots, altered bowel and bladder function, and lymphedema.[27]

Hormone Therapy

Hormone therapy falls into two broad groups: those that block the body's ability to produce hormones and those that interfere with how hormones behave in the body. This type of therapy is used to treat prostate cancer and breast cancer. Whether or not this treatment is used depends on the type of cancer, how far it has spread in the body, and other health problems because it slows or stops the cancer that uses

---

[25] https://www.mayoclinic.org/tests-procedures/radiation-therapy/about/pac-20385162
[26] https://www.mayoclinic.org/tests-procedures/radiation-therapy/about/pac-20385162
[27] https://www.mayoclinic.org/diseases-conditions/cancer/in-depth/cancer-survivor/art-20045524

hormones to grow. Hormone therapy may be given orally, through injection, and by surgery.[28]

Typical side effects include: diarrhea, nausea, fatigue, blood clots, hot flashes, mood changes, weight gain, vaginal dryness, menopausal symptoms, osteoporosis, enlarged and tender breasts, sexual side effects, and increased risk of other cancers.[29]

Immunotherapy

Immunotherapy is a form of biological therapy that uses substances made from living organisms to treat cancer. The immune system was designed to detect and destroy abnormal cells in the body. It can also prevent or slow down the growth of many types of cancer.

Different types of immunotherapies include: immune checkpoint inhibitors, T-cell transfer therapy, monoclonal antibodies, treatment vaccines, and immune system modulators.

Immunotherapy can be given in different ways: intravenous (IV), oral, topical, and intravesical.[30]

Typical side effects include: joint or muscle problems, pain, swelling and weight gain, soreness, redness, itchiness, rash, flu-like symptoms, heart palpitations, sinus congestion, diarrhea, infection, and organ inflammation. Although rare, some types of therapy may cause severe or fatal allergic and inflammation-related reactions.[31]

Targeted Therapy

Targeted therapy targets proteins that control how cancer cells grow, divide, and spread. Most targeted therapies are either small-molecule drugs (small enough to target inside cells) or monoclonal antibodies (proteins produced in a lab designed to attached to certain types of cancer). Targeted therapy can help treat cancer by interfering with specific proteins that help tumors grow and spread throughout the body.

_____

[28] https://www.cancer.gov/about-cancer/treatment/types/hormone-therapy

[29] https://www.mayoclinic.org/diseases-conditions/cancer/in-depth/cancer-survivor/art-20045524

[30] https://www.cancer.gov/about-cancer/treatment/types/immunotherapy

[31] https://www.cancer.gov/about-cancer/treatment/types/immunotherapy/side-effects

Typical side effects include: problems with blood clots and wound healing, heart and vascular problems, high blood pressure, fatigue, mouth sores, nail changes, loss of hair color, and skin problems (rash or dry skin). Very rarely, a hole might form through the wall of the esophagus, stomach, small intestine, large bowel, rectum, or gallbladder. Most side effects go away after treatment ends.[32]

Late Effects of Childhood Cancer

Late side effects of childhood cancer include: heart problems (including a higher risk of heart attack), blood vessel problems (including a higher risk of stroke), lung problems (which can cause difficulty breathing), liver problems, kidney problems, cataracts, bone problems (such as joint pain and bone thinning, also called osteoporosis), short stature (caused by slow bone growth), obesity, infertility, memory loss and learning disabilities, vision loss, hearing loss, thyroid problems, nerve damage, and increased risk of other types of cancers.[33]

Because some of these problems are age related, a person treated for cancer may not realize these problems are related to past cancer treatment(s).

---

[32] https://www.cancer.gov/about-cancer/treatment/types/targeted-therapies
[33] https://www.mayoclinic.org/diseases-conditions/cancer/in-depth/cancer-survivor/art-20045524

The Truth About Healing

Nearly all health problems, no matter what form they take or whatever name they have been given by the medical establishment, are caused by a lack of harmony, imbalances and unresolved issues, past or present, in the emotional body. In order to heal the body, you must first heal the deep-seated feelings that cause the disturbances. When harmony in the emotional body is restored, the body will align easily and the healing you seek will become permanent. — Aurelia Louise Jones[34]

Doctors do not heal. They practice medicine. Pills do not heal. They manage symptoms. True healing comes from within, and it is permanent.

All physical problems, even if they appear to be accidents, have their roots in the mental and emotional bodies. Mental stress and mental illness are rooted in the mental body. Judgment, abandonment, betrayal, fear, sadness, grief, despair, shame, blame, and guilt are rooted in the emotional body.

Each person has his or her own unique and different issues to heal, and because our issues are different, no two people heal in the same way.

The desire to heal is the first and most important step in healing. Ask yourself: "Do I really want to heal? What am I getting out of this dis-ease? What am I afraid to lose or leave behind if I heal? Is what I am doing really worth it in the long run?

What you gain in one area, you lose in another. What you may gain in attention by having a dis-ease, you lose in self-respect. Is it worth the price?

Believing that healing is possible is the next step. When you have a burning desire within your heart to heal and you believe (no doubt) that anything is possible, miracles can and will take place.

---

[34] The Seven Sacred Flames, by Aurelia Louise Jones © 2007 by Mount Shasta Light Publishing. All rights reserved.

Your Higher Self knows exactly what you need to learn and accomplish to meet goals set for each lifetime. True and permanent healing takes place when all of our bodies are balanced.

Someone who has cancer will pay a small fortune to heal using conventional medicine's methods, but the emotional aspect which caused the dis-ease is rarely addressed. Additional stress and trauma are added to an already weakened body.

There is a lesson behind every dis-ease. Removing a body part may temporarily solve the problem. But if the lesson behind the dis-ease has not been learned, the dis-ease will reappear in other organs or body parts until the lesson is learned.

The word "remission" means reduction or decrease. When cancer goes into remission, it does not mean the dis-ease was released. It means the dis-ease may come back. Learn the lesson of the dis-ease so it will not return.

If the lesson was ignored or not learned and the person ends up dying, the dis-ease will take place again in another lifetime, again and again, until the lesson is learned.

For true healing to take place, the past and the present must be healed. As your body begins to let go of pain and suffering, the healing you desire will become permanent.

The Root of Every Illness

Master Hilarion, founder of monasticism in Palestine, lived from 290-371 AD. Monasticism is the practice of devoting one's frugal and secluded life to service. Master Hilarion was a great healer who helped people by resolving and understanding their problems. During his lifetime he performed many miracles. People would come by the thousands for his healings.

Master Hilarion taught that at the root of every illness lies an emotion or a negative way of thinking. Dis-ease is created in the physical body through our misuse of free will and our lack of self-mastery over the emotional, mental, spiritual, and physical bodies. Physical pain and mental distress reflect the emotional pain that needs to be healed and fears that need to be transformed in the conscious mind.

Whether it is a result of an illness or injury, all dis-ease is the result of an emotion or negative way of thinking. For example, when we feel like we're falling down in life, we may fall down physically to reflect what we are feeling inside. Just because we may not be living up to our own expectations does not mean we have failed. Turn the situation around through positive thinking.

If someone were to cut him or herself while paring potatoes, he or she may have been thinking negatively about someone or something. Someone may have hurt this person, and he or she may be wallowing in self-pity as a result. If we do not learn to detach from our emotions, we will drown in them.

When one body is out of balance, all other bodies are out of balance, too. Before healing can take place in the physical body, the mental and emotional bodies must first be healed. Healing is not complete if the focus is only on healing the physical body.

Emotions, false beliefs, and negative ways of thinking can become trapped in the subconscious and unconscious mind from many, many lifetimes. Conscious and subconscious fears hold us back from experiencing love. False beliefs and distorted patterns need to be addressed, released, and healed.

For true healing to take place, we must peel away the many layers we have built up that keep us from experiencing and becoming our true selves. We are like an onion with many layers to peel back to get to the essence of who we really are. That essence is pure unconditional love. Some of these layers go deep, but all must be healed.

Sometimes when it appears everything has been worked out, the issue may come back up again, only to be healed on a deeper level. Healing often seems endless. Past incarnations need to be healed, not just the present one. It may seem worse at the time, but what is being healed is actually less than it was before. Keep working to heal yourself. We all have so many lifetimes that need healing!

What is Dis-Ease?

In order to fully understand healing, dis-ease must also be understood. Energy is always in motion, and the amount of energy flowing through the body will determine the amount of well-being or dis-ease within the body.

Energy can become "stuck" in the spirit body, the result of a fear or negative way of thinking. When dis-ease is present in the spirit body, it is mirrored in the physical body. The spirit body is often called the "body double" because it is identical to the physical body. The spirit body resides within the physical body and gives the physical body what we call "life." You know a spirit is no longer residing within a body when you see a corpse. There is no life in the body.

True healing takes place when all of the four lower bodies are healed and balanced. These four bodies include:

The Mental Body is where we hold our thoughts. While our words validate our thoughts, our thoughts are more powerful than our words because we can lie with our tongues. Our beliefs are important and can be brought in from past lives. For example, someone having difficulty finding a lasting love relationship may have taken a vow of celibacy in a past life. To heal the mental body, we must change our negative way of thinking and the beliefs attached to those thoughts.

The Emotional Body is where we hold every feeling ever experienced—good and bad, past and present, lifetime after lifetime— until it is released. To heal the emotional body, we must release the negative feelings stored therein.

The Spirit Body holds the shock and pain of any trauma, hurt, or memory not released within 18-24 hours. Every body part and organ represents a different type of emotional hurt. When the stored emotion is too much for the spirit body to handle, the emotion will be mirrored in the physical body as pain or dis-ease for you to examine and release.

The Physical Body is nothing but a shell for the mental, emotional, and spirit bodies. When one body heals, it affects the others. When one body is out of balance, all other bodies are affected. When all three bodies are healed, the healing automatically flows into the physical body for complete healing. The breaking down of the physical body eventually creates death. Death takes place when the will to live no longer exists. There is no purpose in life.

The more positive, loving, and peaceful you are, the happier and healthier you will be. The more negative and fearful you are, the more dis-ease will be created to show you what is going on within.

Together the Mind, Body, and Spirit Work to Create Either Well-being or Dis-ease

Every part of the body tells us what is going on within us on a deeper level. The way in which the physical body is cared for will determine how well the body functions and whether or not it will break down in life. Pure love expresses perfect health while negativity or fear express poor health.

Everything begins with a thought, which comes from the mind or mental body, and is reflected back to us through the physical body and in the way we live our life. When our minds are clear and happy, we automatically choose what is best for us on all levels—mentally, emotionally, physically, and spiritually.

The physical body breaks down for many different reasons beyond lack of sleep or poor nutrition. It can break down as a result of negative thoughts, false beliefs, and too little or too much emotion. It can run out of energy, and it can stop working if it doesn't get enough oxygen. Body parts can stop functioning, putting strain on other body parts.

Taking care of our bodies is our responsibility. The choices we make in our everyday life will result in well-being or dis-ease.

Change

We all want life to be different than it is, but too often we don't want to do the work to make it different. We want change to happen on its own. But first we must understand that, like healing, change begins inside and moves outward. Change begins with each individual. We cannot change anyone else, but we can change ourselves, and when we change, our world will change with us.

Change takes place gradually, with intention and courage. Change brings about spiritual growth. It brings about maturity.

Unless you have a burning desire within to bring about change, it simply will not happen. And you are the only one who can make it happen.

You are A Creator!

There is nothing I cannot do. I AM provider. I can provide for self and any others that I wish or desire to. I AM obtainer. There is nothing I cannot obtain if I but wish or desire to. I AM shaper of myself. I AM able to cause myself to be that which I desire to be. I AM former of self. No one causes me to be save self. I AM captain of my own ship, which includes relationships. I AM captain of self. I AM dream maker. I AM able to take my dreams and desires and bring them into reality. I AM Creator. I Create. So it is uttered, so it is. ~ All There Is, Was, and Ever Shall Be through Elliott Eli Jackson[35]

You are a creator. What you think, believe, speak, and feel, you create. When you change your beliefs (your perspectives on life), you change what happens in your life.

Everything begins with a thought. Thoughts are things. The more we think of something, the more attention we give it, the more we create it. The more we believe something to be true, the faster we bring it into existence.

When thoughts are negative, the result is fear. When thoughts are positive, the result is love.

We all came to this school called Earth to be co-creators with God. We came to expand the Light and Love of the world, not the fear we see in it. Your I AM Presence (that spark of God living within you) and God (the Great I AM) work together to create your world.

Watch your words! The spoken word can lift someone up or tear them down. The same is true for us. We put ourselves down without ever realizing the damage taking place.

---

[35] *The I Am Mantras* by Elliott Eli Jackson, channel for All There Is, Was, and Every Shall Be. All rights reserved.

When we use the words, "I am," we call on God, the Great I Am, to help us create the word immediately following "I am." In other words, when you say, "I am poor," you are calling on God to create a situation of poverty. When you say, "I am sick," you are calling on God to create an illness within you. When you say the words, "I am," you are making a statement about who you really are.

Affirmations work to create a condition or modify a behavior as long as the belief is in agreement with the thought. When the two are not in agreement, we stop saying the affirmation, thus stopping the creative process.

Decrees are more powerful because we call on God, the Great I AM, to help create a condition or modify our behavior. A decree always begins with the words "I Am."

Whatever word—negative or positive—following the words "I am" is the desired outcome you are asking God to create with you. Instead of focusing on what you don't want in life (fear), focus on what you do want (love). Call on the Great I AM to help you create a positive condition rather than a negative one.

If physical healing is your intention, say, "I Am healing every day in every way." If emotional healing is your intention, say, "I Am getting stronger every day in every way."

Your world was created through thought. Your words, actions, and beliefs validate your thoughts. Change your thoughts to change your world.

A Closed Mind Will Never Know Truth

Nutrition is at the root of all good health. Health is the state of being free from dis-ease, illness, or injury.

Doctors only know what they have been taught. Most doctors have taken 0-1 courses in nutrition and 0 classes in natural healing while in school. Nutrition classes are not required to receive a medical degree. A survey of 258 family medicine residency programs found "the degree of nutrition knowledge has been found to be low among physicians in practice (20), including family physicians (21)." [36]

In fact, if a medical student does not practice with a pharmaceutical-base protocol, he/she runs the risk of getting kicked out of the program in school. Doctors push pills/medication. In other words, doctors cannot make money if their patients are healthy.

Prescription drugs contain chemicals or unnatural substances to treat an illness that alter the brain chemistry, hormones, or mentality. They appear to work because they trick the brain into thinking something other than what we are experiencing. In other words, the brain does not send communication to the nerves, thus creating the feeling that everything is fine when it may not be.

Medical results are based on treatments and pharmaceuticals experienced by other people—not you! Do not listen to what others have experienced or you can create it. Don't let what other people experienced affect the outcome of your experience. You are unique and different.

To change your health, you must be an active participant in your health care. You are your own best advocate. If your doctor is not with you on your journey, fire them. You do not need someone who does not want to help you.

When looking for a doctor who is best for you, ask if the practice has any vegetarian doctors. A doctor who is vegetarian can teach a plant-based diet. A doctor who eats healthy will support you.

Everything we need to heal is in Nature whether it be a plant, water, tree, rocks, or in the soil. Healing with Nature is *always* best. My rule: "If God made it, use it. God knows everything. If man made it, question it. Man is still learning."

As long as you are talking about a dis-ease, you have not released it. Be careful. You can draw it to you, the result of your desire for attention. If cancer returns, either the lesson wasn't learned the first time or healing on a deeper level is required. It's that simple!

---

[36] http://ebenalexander.com/blog/

Be Honest with Yourself

Everyone and everything in life is a mirror back to us. When someone pushes your buttons or upsets you, it is not that person you are really mad at—you are mad at yourself. You drew that challenging situation to you because of a lesson you needed to learn.

No one can hurt you unless you allow them to do so. If you feel pain (physical or emotional), you may be receiving what you once gave out. When an outcome is not what you expected or when you don't get the attention you crave, you hurt inside. You may feel pain because someone disappointed you. In other words, you didn't accept that person for who they really are.

Look honestly at your role in a situation so you can see what is really taking place.

True Healing: A Spiritual Perspective

Research scientists and doctors look to the physical body for answers; rarely do they look at what is taking place emotionally in a patient's life. If one is only looking at the physical body to diagnose an illness, he/she is missing the bigger picture.

Sometimes dis-ease is a way to leave the body. We chose an exit plan before we came into this incarnation. If the onset of dis-ease was fast (such as cancer or a heart attack) and death was quick, most likely it was a way that person chose to leave the earth plane. If a person lingered awhile before dying, he or she may have been balancing karma before leaving, or had unfinished business to take care of, or may have been given an opportunity to forgive.

Or maybe the lesson was for those around the afflicted person to learn compassion, patience, acceptance, forgiveness, etc. Or maybe those around the person are balancing karma by taking care of that person. There are many reasons and explanations. Each situation is unique and different. Just know that everything happens for a reason and a purpose.

God gave us free will. This means we choose the manner in which we experience dis-ease and the manner in which we heal. We choose what we will accept and what we won't, what we will believe and what we won't. When fear enters the picture, it holds us captive. We become paralyzed. Fear is the only thing that stops us from moving forward in life. It can also take our life.

Everything Spiritual is Simple, Including Healing

True healing cannot begin until you accept responsibility for your role in the situation. Sometimes a dis-ease is karmic. Sometimes we brought it on through our beliefs, words, and actions. A dis-ease may also be something we chose to experience to learn something from. For example, a person who has lost a limb is learning inner strength and perseverance. A lesson not learned will be repeated.

Stand back and be the observer. Look at the situation from another perspective. Look at the whole picture, not just what you want to see. What was your role in creating the situation? What lesson were you learning?

Think of a glass with water and air in it. The glass represents the relationship between the two people, and the water and air represent the two people. When water is added or removed from the glass, doesn't the air automatically change? You cannot change anyone else, but when you change, they will change with you.

In order for your life to change, you must be willing to change. And when you shift your way of thinking and begin to see things differently, your world and those in it will change with you.

"Self" Healing

Modern science will never understand what true healing is and how to achieve it until they begin to understand the spirit body. Science and spirituality are one and can never be separated.

Over time we have forgotten that our bodies were designed to be self-healing. Hair grows and regenerates. Each hair has its own follicle, and each follicle grows new cells, rests for a period of time, then begins the growth process again. The human body is so amazing it can program the hair to grow a certain length, depending on where it is on the body.

The human body continually renews and restores itself. The body we had seven years ago may look the same but most of its cells have been replaced by new ones.

Everyone has the innate ability to heal themselves. Yet at some point we came to believe that some illness or injury we were suffering was more than our bodies could handle, so off we went in search of health care.

Doctors treat the physical body while wholistic practitioners treat the mental, emotional, and spirit bodies. All dis-ease begins with an emotion. The medical establishment views stress as an emotion, and science has proven stress can make us sick. But there are a multitude of other emotions besides stress that can make us sick. Go within to look at the fear behind the emotion. There is always a fear. Release the emotion and move through the fear so the physical body can heal itself.

"Self" Mastery

True and permanent healing takes place when the cause and core of the condition are removed at inner levels.

Mentally, we can pretend a trauma or incident didn't happen, or we can push the trauma to the back of our mind so it becomes inactive. But when something current triggers that old thought or emotion and it resurfaces, dis-ease is apt to manifest again. No permanent healing of the mind or body can result without effort and a change in behavior.

Miracles occur when we draw in a sufficient amount of Light energy to transform a condition of imperfection (fear) into perfection (love). Light substance, or qualified energy, dispels the doubts held in the mental body into the feeling or emotion necessary to dispel depression and disharmony, and into the physical body to restore it by bringing new life.

Through faith, everyone has the ability to heal themselves. Faith is having the courage to believe, with no doubt, in a positive outcome. Faith is the substance of things hoped for and the evidence of things not yet seen. Blind faith is not enough to manifest a cure. Action must be behind faith.

Trust in God to know you will always be taken care of. If you cannot recognize the way in which God speaks to you, you will never hear the answer, and you will never be able to accept the help that may come through someone else.

Trust in yourself to know you have the power within to do anything you really want to do. You simply have to BELIEVE and KNOW without a doubt that healing is possible.

You can receive all the wisdom and guidance necessary to help you heal, but if you do not do the work, it will not happen.

True healing is "self" mastery—understanding the inner causes of the dis-ease. It is learning to master an emotion instead of allowing it to master us. When you work to change your way of thinking, your beliefs, and your emotional state of being, then and only then can true healing occur. True healing takes place when one chooses not to re-create the same conditions.

How to Help Others Heal

Often when a loved one has a dis-ease, we tend to sympathize with them. Sympathy (the sharing of feelings with another) is a negative quality because the distress of the dis-ease becomes amplified in the afflicted person.

Empathy is the ability to understand what someone is experiencing based on your own personal experience. You have "walked a mile" in their shoes. You can relate to what they are experiencing. Instead of feeling sorry for that person, uplift their spirit and move him or her into a better space.

Compassion (a desire to alleviate the suffering) and mercy (compassion shown toward someone) are positive qualities. With compassion and mercy, we witness or become aware of the condition but do not allow the feeling to take control of our heart.

Someone who is not willing to help him or herself cannot heal. If someone cannot accept responsibility for what he or she created, that person is not ready to heal.

Do not be an enabler. It is a misuse of power. An enabler is someone who promotes a specific type of negative behavior in another person (and who loses his or her self-respect in the process).

Worry, fear, and anxiety are negative qualities and can only heighten the dis-ease. When you worry about a loved one, you only make things worse for them by projecting your fear into their energy field, even if solely through thought. This fear lowers their vibration, making his or her situation more difficult to overcome.

The best way to help a loved one to heal is to help him or her stay positive. You can do this by sending them love. Love is the only thing that heals. Help your loved one to see a brighter picture, to see the beauty of life, to find joy in life, and to laugh again. Laughter is the best medicine.

Visualize your loved one surrounded in magenta (unconditional love) or green (healing) light. Visualize the afflicted area healing and returning to a state of perfect health. Visualize how happy he or she will be when they have been healed. Give gratitude in advance for the healing taking place. The more you do this, the faster they will heal.

The Human Body

The following excerpt is from the book, *The Sapiential Discourses: Universal Wisdom, Book 3*, pages 169-171, by All There Is, Was, and Ever Shall Be through Elliott Eli Jackson:

The human mind has great power. At one time we were able to complete certain tasks with only the power of the mind. We could levitate and move objects of different sizes and mass in any direction or from one place to another by using our minds or thought transference, led by the spiritual aspect of our beings. We could transfer thoughts or ideas to another human or animal and cause accelerated healing within and withon the body to other humans, animals, or any portion of the natural landscape of the Earth. We could assist plants and crops with their growth processes, and we could dematerialize at will (bi-locate) as far as 156 miles away.

The human body was not designed to eat more meats than vegetables. The tooth structure of a human is different from that of a carnivore. Humans did not eat meat on a regular basis until approximately 2.1 million years ago, and they did not consume dairy products until about thirteen thousand years ago. The body adjusted to eating meat over time for survival purposes.

The human brain was able to function with certain levels of acids obtained from a high intake of vegetables. They contain very little protein and fat and have different levels of vitamins. The vitamins needed to sustain the proper levels for advanced functions within the brain are found more in vegetables than in meat. Vegetables fight off bone loss, hearing loss, heart disease, diabetes, and all forms of cancer. Without vegetables, the mind and body cannot function at optimum levels.

The human brain today has slowed down over time due to the shift from eating primarily vegetables to consuming both vegetables and meat. Humans today use only approximately 8.76 percent of the brain's capacity. The loss of much of our brain's power was due to a change in nutritional intake.

The Sapiential Discourses, Universal Wisdom, Book II reminds us, "Due to the human body's evolutionary process, the inclusion of meat over an extended period of time has made the human body unable to fully regain the higher mental vibrational level of the past without meat. All of you have created such. Let the hearer hear! This means that it will take an extended period of time—at least five decades—for your human bodies to adjust to the consumption of no meat. However, higher mental function can be regained to a certain extent with the continued consumption of some meat."

For those who are vegetarians, it would be a good idea to consider adjusting your diets. Meat in small quantities is beneficial to the body. The body needs this protein to function properly.

It would be for the highest good of all for us to increase our intake of the following proteins of the highest quality available: kale, peas, sunflower seeds, avocados, bananas, carrots, brown rice, cabbage, broccoli, walnuts, molasses, whole grain products, corn, plantains, potatoes, cantaloupe, and flaxseed.

It would be good to increase our levels of zinc, magnesium, vitamins C, B6, and B12, and niacin, and limit the amount of seaweed. It would also be for our highest good to decrease the use of the following: alcohol, saturated and trans fats, sugar, and prescription medications.

As we adapt to regaining lost functions by adjusting our diets, our abilities will increase in physical speed, stamina, length of life, and memory. We will be able to use lucid dreaming more effectively, and our memory will improve with meditation. We will be able to use our brain to change outcomes, and the use of levitation for comfort and production purposes will increase. Telepathic communication, astral projection, telekinesis, thought transference, and other lost functions will return.

The Fourfold Body

Happily today, the spiritual aspect of your being is now being taken seriously. Look now at the treatment of cancer. In your society now, many programs that deal with cancer place heavy attention on the spiritual for healing and recovery—as well they should, we may add. Your medical communities will never be able to effectively heal cancer and many other diseases until they fully accept the importance of addressing and integrating the spiritual portion of you within their modalities for treatment and recovery. ~ All There Is, Was, and Ever Shall be through Elliott Eli Jackson[37]

The physical body was designed to be self-healing. It does not naturally wear out or break down due to age as we have been taught. The human body breaks down because of the way we live life.

The mental, emotional, spiritual, and physical bodies work together in unison. When one is out of balance, all are out of balance (domino effect). To achieve and maintain well-being, all bodies must be cared for. (See Appendix, How to Care for Your Fourfold Body.)

When we change, our world and our physical body change with us.

The Mental Body

The mental body is oval in shape and extends around the spirit body, holding our thoughts and ideas. Its function is to create and hold a vision until physical manifestation can take place. The mental body, or vehicle of consciousness known as the "mind," has a language of its own—not of words, but of colors, sounds, and forms. The physical brain carries out what the mind desires.

---

[37] The Sapiential Discourses: Universal Wisdom, by All There Is, Was, and Ever Shall Be through Elliott Eli Jackson © 2012 by Light Technology Publishing. All rights reserved.

All of life and everything that happens in it began with a thought. Thoughts go through our mind every second of every day, and these thoughts are influenced by many forces outside and within us, which affect our personality.

Outside forces include the position of the sun, moon, and planets in the sky (astrology), and the position of the earth in our galaxy. Our thoughts are influenced by the collective consciousness of the country and the times we live in, by the people who prepare our food and by the people with whom we work and socialize. They are influenced by what our family, friends, and peers think and expect of us, and by the way we are raised. Our thoughts are influenced by our ethnicity, race, culture, gender, disability, and religious background.

Inside forces include our own level of consciousness, our beliefs, what we think of ourselves, our self-worth, and by what we have done in the past (present and past incarnations). Our beliefs from the past have an influence on the present.

If you have ever tried to meditate, you know how difficult it is to shut down your thoughts. Thoughts come and go all day long—and sometimes all night long. Some thoughts are repetitive, some are incoherent, and some are gone as quickly as they came. Everything begins with a thought. All of life began with a thought in the mind of God.

A thought becomes powerful once a belief is attached to it. Our beliefs are formed as a result of our experiences (present and past incarnations). The more we believe something, the more emotion we invest in it, and this powerful combination of thought and feeling inevitably influences the actions we take.

Energy follows attention. The more attention we give something, the more we create it. The more we believe in something, the faster we bring it into fruition. Thoughts are catchy.

If we think about living a life centered on love, if we believe in such a life, then we can create it for ourselves. When we live a life rooted in love, we live a long and healthy life. If our life is rooted in fear, our bodies break down and we begin to experience dis-ease.

When you place your faith and trust outside of yourself, thinking someone else knows more than you or are better than you, you give that person your power. They grow stronger, and you grow weaker. Their ego is fed while your self-esteem slips away.

A simple thought can uplift someone, or it can tear them down. Thoughts are things, and every thought will come back to its source in the positive or negative manner in which it was given out, tenfold.

Your world was created by your thoughts. If you don't like your world, change your way of thinking. Changing your thoughts can be difficult, but it is doable and well worth it in the long run.

The Emotional Body

Know that all physical problems, even if they appear to be accidents, always have their roots in the emotional and mental bodies. Mental stress and mental illnesses also have their roots in the emotions. The emotional body is the most important area to begin with for your healing. – Discourse from Master Adama with Master Hillarion[38]

The emotional body is the largest of the four lower bodies. Like the mental body, it, too, is oval in shape and extends at least three feet out from the physical body. It contains the feelings, positive and negative, from our present and former embodiments. Its function is to radiate the nature of the God force—every virtue of happiness, patience, humility, purity, mercy, wisdom, love, forgiveness, and peace; not to radiate violent feelings, which manifest in war or imperfection of any kind.

The emotional body fuels the thoughts. Energy follows attention. The more we focus our energy on something, the more we let our energy flow into it. The more attention we give someone or something—even a thought—the more energy we grant it. The world as we know it was created by our collective thoughts, past and present. Emotion is the fuel used to bring thoughts into reality.

The emotional body holds every feeling ever experienced—good and bad, past and present, lifetime after lifetime—until it is released. To heal the emotional body, we must release the negative feelings stored therein.

---

[38] *The Seven Sacred Flames*, by Aurelia Louise Jones © 2007 by Mount Shasta Light Publishing. All rights reserved.

The more positive, loving, and peaceful we are, the happier and healthier we will be. The more negative and fearful we are, the more dis-ease will be created to show us what is really going on within.

The Spirit Body

External pains and difficulties are always the mirrors of inner pains and fears. They mirror to you what needs to be healed and transformed in your consciousness. – Discourse from Master Adama with Master Hilarion[39]

The spirit or spirit body, often called the body double, resembles the physical body in shape and extends 4-6 inches around the physical body. It is composed of tiny channels of energy, called nadis ("tube" or "pipe" in Hindi.) These nadis connect at certain points of intensity called chakras. They are the counterparts of the physical nervous system. The spirit body contains the memories (actions, thoughts, and feelings) of all our experiences from former embodiments. The accumulated record of these experiences is called the soul.

The spirit body is very complex, consisting of many different layers unseen to the naked eye. Each body contains an aura, chakras, and meridians. The physical eye sees only the physical body. While there are people who can see auras and chakras with the physical eyes, the different spirit bodies and meridians remain unseen.

The spirit body holds the shock and pain of any trauma, hurt, or memory not released within 18-24 hours. Every body part and organ represents a different type of emotional hurt. When the stored emotion is too much for the spirit body to handle, the emotion will be mirrored in the physical body as pain or dis-ease for you to examine and release.

The majority of pain is held in the spirit body, not the physical body. To release pain, one must release the emotional pain causing the dis-ease in the body.

---

[39] *The Seven Sacred Flames*, by Aurelia Louise Jones © 2007 by Mount Shasta Light Publishing. All rights reserved.

The Physical Body

You have many types of bodies, what you call various subtle bodies. You also have four main body systems; the physical vehicle, the emotional body, the mental body, and the spirit body. ... They work together; when you suppress one, you suppress the others. When you heal one, you bring relief to the others as well. When you ingest or inhale toxic chemical substances into your body, be aware that there are certain types of substances that are fairly easy to eliminate from the body, and others for which the body has no mechanism of elimination.
– Discourse from Master Adama with Master Hilarion[40]

The physical body is the temple for the spirit that lives within. It is also the temple for the spark of God, which is anchored in the heart of your physical body. How you take care of your physical body will determine what it will look like at the close of an incarnation.

Every thought, belief, and emotion that is important to you is held in the spirit body and is reflected in the physical body. The physical body is a wonderful instrument to demonstrate what is going on within our mental and emotional bodies. We can lie to ourselves about the way we feel emotionally, but our physical body never lies. All dis-ease is an indication that our thoughts are out of alignment with our Higher Self.

The physical body allows us to live in the physical world and acts as an anchor to the Earth. The brain is the organ in the physical body through which the mind works. It registers impressions from the outer world. The nervous system functions like a network of fine wires, bearing messages—thoughts and feelings—as electrical impulses to all parts of the body. The main conduit is the spinal cord, which works constantly. The descending arc of electrical energy anchors the body to the surface of the Earth, and the powerful ascending current enables us to stand erect and move about rather than to crawl on the ground. The skeletal system is the foundation on which the body is built. Beliefs are held in the bones.

---

[40] *The Seven Sacred Flames*, by Aurelia Louise Jones © 2007 by Mount Shasta Light Publishing. All rights reserved.

The physical body is the vehicle used by the spirit, or Lower Self, to maneuver through life. The spirit lives within the physical body, and the spirit is responsible for what happens to the physical body just as you are responsible for your car and what happens to it.

The physical body is nothing but a shell for the mental, emotional, and spirit bodies. When one body heals, it affects the others. When one body is out of balance, all other bodies are affected. When all three bodies are healed, the healing automatically flows into the physical body for complete healing. The breaking down of the physical body eventually creates death. Death takes place when the will to live no longer exists. There is no purpose in life.

There are many pains we experience for which no medical diagnosis can be made. For example, the pain someone feels after they've lost a limb. Doctors call it "phantom pain," but that pain is real to the person who has lost the limb. They may have lost the limb in their physical body, but they did not lose the limb in their spirit body.

Most pain is held in the spirit body, not the physical body. Pain is either mental or emotional and, therefore, has its roots in the mental or emotional body. When the pain becomes more than we can handle, it flows into the physical body to show us what is going on within.

Thoughts Create

The brain controls every aspect of the physical body and sends signals or messages through the nerves to various parts and systems of the body. It tells the body what to do or what not to do. It's like the body's central computer.

The brain is also the vehicle of the mind, or mental body. It records everything that goes on within and around it continuously. It records all thoughts, beliefs, memories, and experiences, both good and bad, from all lifetimes. The brain processes everything, consciously or subconsciously.

The physical body is made up of atoms. One atom is made up of many electrons vibrating at different speeds, all orbiting a central core called a nucleus. There is distance between each electron. As the electrons swing through their orbit, light expands or decreases (a result of discord). These electrons create form through thought. The pattern for the vibratory rate is determined by the level of emotion pouring through the electrons.

These electrons create form through thought. The pattern for the vibratory rate is determined by the level of emotion pouring through the electrons. When our thoughts, feelings, and subconscious memories focus on negativity or fear, the vibratory rate of the electrons is slowed down and the vibratory rate of our four lower bodies lowers. The lower the vibration, the more we open ourselves to dis-ease, poverty, depression, and all other negative aspects of life.

When our thoughts, feelings, and subconscious memories focus on positivity or love, the vibratory rate of the electrons is increased, and the vibratory rate of our four lower bodies rises. The higher the vibration, the more we open ourselves to health and well-being, abundance and prosperity, joy, love and peace, and all other positive aspects of life.

Keys to Life: Balance and Moderation

Our inner world represents our feeling world, and our outer world represents what we project to the world around us. When our inner and outer worlds are out of balance, our outer world will reflect the opposite of our inner world. For example, a bully displays a powerful persona outwardly so that no one will see how weak he or she is on the inside.

Co-dependent relationships are always out of balance. On the surface, one person may appear to have all the power while the other person may appear to have little or none but take a closer look and you will find this is not the case. In truth, both parties are getting something out of the relationship or they wouldn't stay in it.

When we put someone on a pedestal, we give that person our power. This type of relationship is out of balance because one person's ego grows stronger, while the other's self-esteem grows weaker. The more we give our power away, the weaker we become until eventually we feel we have nothing—no power, no control, no self-esteem, and no self-worth.

All relationships must be balanced to be healthy.

Too much (excess) or too little (deprivation) of anything throws life off balance. Without moderation—be it food, exercise, alcohol/drugs—there are no boundaries. Without boundaries, there is no self-respect. Without self-respect, one cannot truly love one's self. It is impossible to truly love another if one cannot love him/herself. Balance and moderation are the keys to life.

Keys to Releasing Cancer and Living Healthy

Quality of life is more important than quantity of life! Live a life that is good for you, one that is healthy, so you can live long. Take good care of yourself so you can save money and do the things you love!

Empower yourself! Knowledge is power. Health is power. Educate yourself in the areas of health and well-being. For example, did you know that cancer drugs have repeatedly been found to make tumors worse and kill the patient more quickly? Yet a multitude of studies have shown that turmeric reduces a tumor's size by an average of 81 percent.[41]

Do your homework. Investigate. The information in this book is just the beginning. There is always more. Expand your knowledge base to know Truth.

---

[41] http://ebenalexander.com/blog/

The Importance of a Healthy Body

The importance of a healthy body cannot be stressed enough. It allows you to live a more active, joyful life. It means you will have a better quality of life as you age.

A healthy body requires a well-balanced and nutritious diet, juicing, drinking mineral and spring water, taking the appropriate vitamins and supplements, exercise, a good cleanse, prayer and meditation, quality sleep at night, and a well-rounded lifestyle.

Learning how to balance stress is also an important part of maintaining a healthy body. One way stress can be released is through breathwork. It can decrease the risk for heart disease, high blood pressure, diabetes, and mental health disorders.

A healthy diet will include proteins, carbohydrates, and fats. A regular routine of exercise will strengthen bones, muscles, lungs, and the cardiovascular system. Seven to eight hours of sleep will allow the body to repair cells and perform other maintenance the body needs.

When we are young, we often take our bodies for granted, but as we get older, we sometimes wish we would have taken better care of our bodies as we aged so we wouldn't feel so miserable as we got older.

If you aren't already taking care of your body properly, it's never too late to start. The investment made to maintain a healthy body will not only decrease the amount of medical bills paid later on in life, but it will also allow more opportunity to do more and enjoy life once retirement age is reached.

Your physical body is only one component that makes up the whole of your being. What you eat and how you take care of your body does have an effect on the physical body, but what you think, say, and do have an even greater effect.

A Well-Balanced Diet

A well-balanced diet provides the energy needed to make it through the day. It consists of all the vitamins, minerals, and nutrients essential to maintain healthy cells, organs, muscle, and tissue. A well-balanced diet supports the cardiovascular and immune systems and assists in weight control.

Foods should be fresh and healthy for your body, free of chemicals and preservatives. Whole grains (not processed grains), beans, and nuts should be eaten. More fish, fowl, and lamb should be eaten than red meats. Leafy green vegetables (raw or steamed) and fruits should be eaten daily.

Milk should be included for calcium and protein. Foods should be rich in Vitamins A, C, and E, selenium, potassium, and fiber. Fried foods and an overabundance of sugars and alcohol should be avoided. A strong, healthy body makes it difficult for dis-ease to settle in.

Edgar Cayce recommended a diet that is 80 percent alkaline to 20 percent acid. It should be noted that just because a food is acid, it does not indicate that it REMAINS acid in the body. It can turn alkaline. Honey and raw sugars produce alkaline ash, but because of the high concentrate of sugar, they become acid-formers. (See Appendix, Acid-Forming and Alkaline-Forming Foods)

Nutrition

The human body is comprised of ten complex systems, each performing a different function to regulate the body. These systems include: skeletal, muscular, nervous, endocrine, cardiovascular, lymphatic, respiratory, digestive, urinary, and reproductive.

There are six basic elements that make up the physical body: carbon, nitrogen, hydrogen, calcium, oxygen, and phosphorus. Other elements (in miniscule amounts) include: sodium, magnesium, sulfur, zinc, copper, molybdenum, selenium, chlorine, iodine, fluorine, cobalt, iron, manganese, lead, lithium, aluminum, strontium, silicon, arsenic, bromine, and vanadium.

Nutrition means eating a healthy diet, full of the nutrients found in fruits and vegetables grown in fertile soil. Green leafy vegetables, such as kale and spinach, are rich in vitamin C and beta carotene.

Black raspberries contain anthocyanins, antioxidants, orac (oxyten radical absorbent capacity), and ellagic acid which stimulates cancer cells to commit suicide all while feeding the brain and the lens of the eye and prevents cancer.

Figs contain phison, an important phytochemical which has been proven to stimulate apoptosis (program cell death in cancer cells).

A Harvard University Study found eating two servings of certain whole fruits a week can reduce the risk of certain types of cancer and lower the risk of type 2 diabetes. Black raspberries, figs, blueberries, apples, grapes, and peaches are high in antioxidants that can assist in programing cell death in cancer.[42]

Four essential nutrients that make up the cornerstones of a healthy diet that keep the physical body in balance and functioning well are water, carbohydrates, fat, and protein.

- Carbohydrates found in plant foods get converted into glucose, providing energy for the physical body.
- Excessive fats cause problems in the body, but a reasonable amount of fat is required to support growth and to provide energy.
- Proteins can be found in meat, fish, eggs, nuts, seeds, beans, dairy products, and other protein sources. They support the muscles, tissues, skin, and major organs.

When we feel positive and loving, we eat healthily (fresh fruits and vegetables, beans, and whole grains). When we feel lousy and think negatively, we tend to eat poorly (fried foods, unnatural foods, and sweets).

The foods we choose to eat and how we prepare our food will determine how well they will be assimilated in the body. Natural foods contribute to optimum health and longevity of the body.

For a healthy body, follow recommended dietary guidelines from The Weston A. Price Foundation's website (www.westonaprice.org). The Weston A. Price Foundation (WAPF) is a source for accurate information on nutrition and health, always aiming to provide the scientific validation of conventional foodways. People seeking health today often condemn certain food groups — such as grains, dairy

---

[42] https://news.harvard.edu/gazette/story/2013/08/reduce-type-2-diabetes-risk/

foods, meat, salt, fat, sauces, sweets and nightshade vegetables — but the Wise Traditions Diet is inclusive, not exclusive.

The Weston A. Price Foundation will show you how to include nourishing conventional foods in your diet through wise choices and proper preparation techniques. The result is vibrant health for every age of life, including the next generation.

Vitamins and Supplements

Every day, take the appropriate vitamins and supplements to support the body. Our land is not as enriched in vitamins and minerals as it once was. Therefore, it is important for everyone to take a daily vitamin and any supplements their body requires. Muscle or body test (also known as the sway test) to see if your body needs a particular supplement. Your body knows what it needs.

At one time in humanity's history, our vibrations were so low that our bodies were mostly carbon based. Over time, our vibrations have risen. Our bodies are now crystalline in nature. In other words, we are human pendulums. You can receive "yes" and "no" answers from your body because your body has a consciousness. It will not lie to you. And yes, this really does work!

To body test, stand straight with your arms hanging loosely at your side. The eyes are the entranceway to the soul. To keep the mind from overriding the answer, close your eyes.

Now ask your body, "Please show me a yes." Note which direction it moved. Now ask your body, "Please show me a no." Note which direction it moved. Remain relaxed, allowing your body to move in whatever direction it desires. Now ask your question(s).

Do not ask questions about the future. The future does not exist. It is constantly changing. You may not receive a correct answer. If the body does not want to move in either direction, you most likely have a fear stopping you, and you are afraid to receive the answer.

It is always best to drink a glass of water about 10-15 minutes before doing this test. Always test your body for your "yes" and "no" answer before asking your body questions. If your body is dehydrated, its polarity will be reversed. Your answers will be correct, but they will be reversed.

Body test to see if a particular brand of vitamin or supplement is best for you. Not all brands are the same. Some are packaged beautifully and are huge in size as a marketing gimmick to sell more vitamins. You think you're getting more, but you're really not.

Body test to see if you should take the vitamin/supplement in the morning or evening and to see if you should you take a gel, liquid, capsule, or pill, in addition to how much of each vitamin/supplement you should take. Dosages on the product label are designed for the average public. Not all of us fit into this category. We are all unique and different.

Vitamins and supplements are needed for the body to break down macronutrients like carbohydrates, fat and protein. They also help our bodies to function; i.e., fight infection, fight off toxins, strengthen bones and teeth, reduce the risk of getting the common cold, maintain healthy skin and tissue, make collagen in our bones, help with wound healing, protect against heart disease, improve muscle function, regulate blood pressure and glucose levels, aids in hormone secretion, improves immune function, increases energy levels, improves brain function and the ability to concentrate, and so much more.[43] In other words, they help to maintain a healthy body. Without them, your body cannot function at its best. Everyone's needs are different.

A proper diet is the best way to maintain good nutrition. Supplements should never be a replacement for healthy eating.

Vitamin C—A Powerful Antioxidant

Dr. Patrick Quillen, former Vice President of Nutrition for Cancer Treatment Centers of American, stated on his website: "Vitamin C can become a targeted anti-cancer agent because it resembles the preferred fuel of cancer, glucose, and is absorbed by cancer cells in abundance. The ascorbic acid by itself in an anaerobic environment then becomes a powerful pro-oxidant and destroys the cancer cell—but only the cancer

---

[43] http://ebenalexander.com/blog/

73

cells, since healthy cells have built-in mechanisms for absorbing the right amount of vitamin C along with the entire "symphony" of other antioxidants.

"There is compelling evidence that high dose intravenous vitamin C (IVC) has a central role in cancer treatment. High dose IVC as sole therapy has often been shown to be effective in advanced cancer patients." [44]

Vitamin C plays a critical role in our health because it is an essential nutrient that the body cannot make. This vitamin is best obtained from a healthy diet. Vitamin C defends the body against cell damage and plays an important role in growing and developing tissues, healing wounds, and keeping your immune system strong.[45]

Eating Organic

The USDA National Organic Program (NOP) defines organic as: Organic food is produced by farmers who emphasize the use of renewable resources and the conservation of soil and water to enhance environmental quality for future generations. Organic meat, poultry, eggs, and dairy products come from animals that are given no antibiotics or growth hormones. Organic food is produced without using most conventional pesticides; fertilizers made with synthetic ingredients or sewage sludge; or ionizing radiation. Before a product can be labeled "organic," a government-approved certifier inspects the farm where the food is grown to make sure the farmer is following all the rules necessary to meet USDA organic standards. Companies that handle or process organic food before it gets to your local supermarket or restaurant must be certified, too." [46]

A truly organic product will have a "100% Organic" logo on the packaging. "Organic" means the product is 95-99 percent organic, and "Made with Organic Ingredients" means the product is 70-94 percent organic.

---

[44] https://beatingcancerwithnutrition.com/vitamin-c-for-cancer-treatment/
[45] https://health.clevelandclinic.org/vitamin-c
[46] http://ebenalexander.com/blog/

According to an April 2012 AARP bulletin, to be able to tell if grocery store produce is truly organic, look at the Price Look Up (PLU) sticker. If the produce is organic, the code will contain five digits beginning with 9 (95023). Non-organic produce will only contain four digits (5023). A five-digit PLU beginning with 8 means the item is genetically modified (85023).[47]

When a product is labeled "Natural," harmful toxins may be used as ingredients. While the best place to get fresh produce is at a local farmer's market, it does not guarantee the produce was grown in an organic environment.

Processed Foods vs. Whole Foods

Processed foods are put through a "process," produced in a manufacturing plant, packaged, and then put on a shelf to be stored until ready to be eaten. Some processed foods contain whole foods, such as peanut butter, dried fruit, bread, canned beans, etc.

Processed foods also contain artificial ingredients (i.e., preservatives, oils, sweeteners, and flavors) to enhance taste and to prolong shelf life. Cooking time is minimal or none. Ingredients include chemicals and other unrecognizable names. If you can't pronounce an ingredient or you don't know what it is, you probably shouldn't be eating it.

Natural or whole foods are grown in orchards, gardens, or greenhouses. They are unprocessed, unrefined, and have a shorter shelf life because they have no artificial ingredients. They are full of vitamins, minerals, antioxidants, phytochemicals, and fiber your body needs to be healthy. The life force in plants helps sustain our life force. Cooking them takes more time, but they are better for the body and soul.

The main difference between the two is Love. Love is not found in processed foods that are factory produced. The more one loves to cook, the greater the love put into the food (home-made). Love makes food

---

[47] http://ebenalexander.com/blog/

taste better. Homemade food fuels the physical body, and the love put into making the food fuels the soul.

Juicing

Many health benefits are derived from drinking freshly juiced fruits and vegetables, and it is a great way to add nutrients from the fruits or vegetables that you normally would not eat.

Juicing extracts the nutrients from fruits and vegetables, making them easier to digest and absorb. It can provide vitamins, minerals, and plant chemicals (phytochemicals) found in the whole versions of those foods. They can also provide antioxidants that support the immune system and have potential anti-cancer properties. When it comes to juicing for releasing cancer, certain fruits and vegetables are particularly beneficial due to their high nutrient content.

Fruit and vegetable juices retain most of the vitamins, minerals and plant chemicals (phytonutrients) found in the whole versions of those foods. These nutrients can help protect against cardiovascular disease, cancer and various inflammatory diseases, like rheumatoid arthritis.

Valuable compounds called flavonoids and anthocyanins are abundant in a variety of fruits and vegetables and guard against oxidative cellular damage, which comes from everyday cellular maintenance and is worsened by exposure to chemicals and pollution.

Make sure you eat enough fiber to keep your digestive system working smoothly. Juice three times a week. The consistency should be that of a smoothie. You can add dissolvable fiber powder to your juices or supplement with a suitable number of fiber-rich solid foods (like prunes or pears) to compensate.

Create your own smoothie containing fruits and vegetables high in anti-cancer properties and packed with antioxidants that can help protect cells from any cell damage. One tasty recipe includes: kale, cucumber, green apple (entire apple: skin, core and seeds, no stem), turmeric root or turmeric, orange, carrot, banana, and blueberries.

Muscle or body test to see which fruits and vegetables, fiber, etc. are best for your body. Your body knows exactly what it needs.

Excellent sources of foods high in vitamins and minerals include:

- Soursop (Graviola)—High in vitamin C, soursop fruit and graviola tree leaves can be used to treat stomach ailments, fever, parasitic infections, hypertension and rheumatism. The principal interest in this plant is because of its strong anticancer effects. Although it is effective for a number of medical conditions, it is its anti-tumor effect that is of the most interest. This plant is a proven cancer remedy for cancers of all types.

- Moringa—This wonderful plant has been used for centuries due to its medicinal properties and health benefits. It has antifungal, antiviral, antidepressant, and anti-inflammatory properties. Moringa extracts contain properties that might help prevent cancer developing. It also contains niazimicin, which is a compound that suppresses the development of cancer cells. Moringa is believed to have many benefits, and its uses range from health and beauty to helping prevent and cure diseases.

  According to *The Moringa Way*, "Moringa contains a variety of cancer-fighting compounds, such as isoquercetin (a compound which inhibits bladder cancer), kaempferol (an antioxidant that is adept at stopping cancerous cells from spreading and reducing inflammation.) and rhamnetin (compound researchers suggest that it's able to kill prostate cancer cells). Another anti-cancerous property called Eugenol is also found in Moringa which makes this plant great anti-cancer medicine for leukemia, bone, liver, gastric, and skin cancer. Moringa also have an anti-tumor capacity due to the benzyl isothiocyanate (studies shown to have anti-cancer and chemoprotective capabilities) that it contains. It's very important for those who are battling cancer as it helps to strengthen cells so that they can tolerate chemotherapy. Besides these, Moringa is still filled with all the vitamins, antioxidants, anti inflammatories, amino acids, antibacterial, and omega fatty acids that all help your body fight cancers and different infections.[48]

- Celery Juice—Celery's juices neutralize and flush toxins from the liver, brings down toxic liver heat, raises hydrochloric acid and helps the liver produce bile.

Juicing is one way to stay healthy. Vegetables fight off bone loss, hearing loss, heart disease, diabetes, and all forms of cancer. Without vegetables, the mind and body cannot function at optimum levels. They are important ingredients to achieve and maintain a healthy body.

Water

The most common substance found on earth is water. Every living thing requires water to survive. The human body is made up of mostly water.

Water is a universal solvent. It is used for drinking, cooking, and bathing. It is used for irrigation and for extinguishing fires. Water is used in homes, buildings, factories, and in fountains. We could not live without water.

Water is important to flush the body of chemicals, toxins, and other waste products it contains. It regulates body temperature and maintains cleanliness by excreting urine and other poisonous substances from the body. It serves as a lubricant for the body, aiding in chewing, swallowing, and moving solids through the body. Water is the best cure for most illnesses.

"Live" Water vs. "Dead" Water

Mineral and spring water are considered "live" water because the life force of the water helps sustain our life force. Both contain electrolytes and other minerals that support all cellular functions.

---

[48]

https://thetruthaboutcancer.com/?fbclid=IwAR3W7pRs338l34KPRPP27M2B5CRK MJpiaTgb3VhnJgPUJ1KFbEjRYRYWOtM

Mineral water comes from a well or mineral spring and contains natural trace minerals important to maintaining well-being. The type of minerals in the water varies from region to region. Mineral water replaces minerals the body naturally loses through the day.

Spring water comes from underground aquifers. The water is clear and has been filtered by solid rock. It, too, contains natural minerals important to the body. Minerals improve the taste of the water.

Purified and distilled water are considered to be "dead" water because all contaminants have been removed, as well as electrolytes and minerals important to the body.

Purified water can come from any source of water, including spring, ground, or tap water. The EPA requires that it meet significantly higher filtration and purification standards than those for regular drinking water (e.g., tap water).

Distilled water is water that has been through a distillation process. It is ideal for applications where minerals can be counterproductive (e.g., machinery and cleaning products). While distilled water is the cleanest bottled water readily available, it is not good for drinking because it pulls minerals out of the bloodstream and other parts of the body.

The Proper Amount of Hydration

Because the human body is approximately seventy to ninety percent water, most people (unless dehydrated) only need to drink four to six cups a day or the body will become oversaturated. What happens when you fill a glass with more water than it can contain? Problems result.

Just as too little water can lead to dehydration, too much water can cause mineral depletion and other imbalances within the body. Too much water can dilute stomach acids causing acid reflux and agitate a hiatal hernia. Too much water combined with a high-fiber diet can lead to bloating, gas, and other digestive disorders. Balance is the key.

Oxygenated Water

Oxygenated water is water that has been injected with extra oxygen under high pressure. Yes, a single breath of air contains more oxygen than a whole bottle of oxygenated water—but our air is polluted. So what else are we breathing in when we take that breath of air?

When oxygen levels are low, cancer cells have more of an opportunity to thrive and multiply. A body high in oxygen can help promote the replication of good bacteria needed to keep our body safe from bad bacteria that will do harm and cause dis-ease. Pathogens are almost never found in oxygen rich environments.

Oxygenated water is good for your skin and health. It can help make your heart and muscles work better, and some say it can improve wrinkles, hair loss, and *even* spider veins. Oxygen is needed in the body for energy to be released from the food molecules. This is called aerobic respiration, and it is the best way to produce energy in the body.

People who drink oxygenated water will get more oxygen into their bloodstream. The two greatest needs of the body are oxygen and water. Without either of these two the body will die.

Activated Stabilized Oxygen (ASO) water is pH balanced, all natural, and full of oxygen molecules. "It is produced using a proprietary engineering process that fuses free oxygen molecules with plant-derived minerals. The result is a better performance supplement that boosts oxygen levels in the body for better energy efficiency, mental clarity, and improved recovery from physical stressors." [49]

A Good Cleanse

The human body should be purged periodically of the many chemicals and minerals for which it should have only trace, if any, amounts. An excess of toxins can slow down the mind, body, and spirit. It can inhibit well-being.

Fasting to cleanse the body should only be done on a limited basis (once or twice a year) for no more than three days. Anything more can be detrimental to your health. During this time, drink only water and eat only raw vegetables to cleanse the blood and to aid your digestive system by removing unnecessary particles that need to be removed.

---

[49] https://www.oxigenesisinc.com/

Exercise

Early shamans in China believed we could all be healthier and live longer if we cultivated the life force within through various exercises, movements (e.g., yoga and tai chi), special diets and herbs, breathing exercises, and meditation.

Go for a walk every day to clear the mind, get fresh air, and exercise. Regular exercise is important for maintaining a healthy weight and for reducing the risk of cardiovascular disease. Spend thirty to sixty minutes, three days a week, on a treadmill or an elliptical machine to strengthen your cardiovascular system.

Moderate exercise includes walking fast for 15 minutes, going for a bike ride, or cleaning the house two to three days a week. A more vigorous form of exercise would include jogging, running, swimming, and most types of competitive sports.

Exercise to keep your body firm and flexible. Use an elliptical or stationary bicycle for a healthy heart.

Your physical body is the vehicle your spirit has been given to enable you to move around in life. If you do not take good care of your vehicle, it will break down.

Prayer and Meditation

Prayer and meditation have a profound effect on your well-being. People who pray and meditate daily have lower stress levels, age less, and live longer, and maintain a state of calm. They are better prepared to handle the trials and tribulations of life.

Through prayer and meditation, you learn patience, forgiveness, hope, faith, trust, love, and true happiness. Your connection to God and all of the Divine strengthens each time you pray and meditate. You know that you are never really alone. You know that you are loved.

Every day, pray out loud so the Universe can respond to your prayers. Every day, give gratitude for what you have in life. Gratitude is the highest vibrational prayer there is. Give gratitude in advance for what you want more of in life (including the releasing of all unnecessary cancer from your entire being), for healing, for perfect health and well-being, and more.

When life throws you a curve ball, give gratitude. The more you give gratitude for something, the more you get of it. Three to five minutes of gratitude will shift you into a positive way of being. Give gratitude in advance for the releasing of all unnecessary cancer or disease taking place.

Give gratitude for life for life is a gift. Treasure it always. Give gratitude whenever you can. Give gratitude for unanswered prayers. Unanswered prayers are quite often prayers that have been answered.

Talk to God out loud. Make it a regular habit. Talk about anything and everything—what you like, what you don't like, what you want out of life. Recognize when your prayer has been answered.

The most effective way to find inner peace and request guidance is through meditation. Take time to go within to find your own answers.

Start your day off with ten minutes of meditation, eyes open, to clear the mind and align your fourfold body. Meditating with the eyes closed is relaxation. Focus on a moving object to help clear unwanted thoughts from the mind. Meditate daily. You'll be surprised how well your day will go!

When one of your bodies is down, they are all down (domino effect). Synchronicity stops when our fourfold being is not in alignment.

Meditate to focus and center one's self, allowing the spinal cord and muscles to be worked on by the universe. Meditation allows the spiritual portion of your being to release. It allows you to look at past situations, behaviors, and actions to see things clearly. During meditation the heart rate and breathing slow down naturally, which slows down the blood flow of all the internal systems, including the brain.

Meditation helps you to become more in tune with parts of your world and other worlds, planes of existence, and time frames. Meditation allows you to open up to endless new possibilities to living life.

There are different ways to meditate: sitting cross-legged on the floor, on a kneeling bench, or sitting in a straight-backed chair. Choose what is best for you. Meditation can also be done in a labyrinth, medicine wheel, or salt cave, or by taking a walk in Nature. Running, gardening, vacuuming, ironing, eating, dancing, walking, and sleeping can all be forms of meditation.

A regular practice of prayer and meditation will help you progress on your spiritual journey. It is a way to open and expand your mind, to stay in touch with your inner self, and to keep you from getting caught up in worldly ways. It will keep darkness away.

Breathe!

For a more joyous outlook on life and to calm the emotions, take time to breathe. God is everywhere, including in the air that we breathe. Take time to breathe in the breath of God, three to four deep cleansing breaths, in through the nose and out through the mouth, at least twice a day.

Empty the lungs of stale breath. Form the mouth into an "oo" sound and breathe out heavily. Stand erect, with your feet together and your arms resting at your sides.

- Slowly inhale to the count of five, raising your arms over your head. As you inhale, push the diaphragm out.
- Hold to the count of five while visualizing a shaft of Golden White Light pouring down from your crown chakra and going through every part of your body and into your energy field.
- Exhale to the count of five, slowly lowering the arms back down to the sides.
- Hold to the count of five.

Repeat this seven times. This is a great way to release stress and bring you back into balance.

Breathe when adversity comes knocking at your door! Take a step back to be the observer. What is really going on? When you feel it in your gut, it's your "stuff." Look at the whole picture, not just what you want to see. Take time to go within. You are in this situation for a reason. What do you need to learn from it? What are your fears? What are you getting out of the situation? Do you have an attachment to the outcome? Are you placing expectations on someone who cannot meet them? Change your perspective. Diffuse the situation and move forward.

Breathe to clear your mind and to let go of stress. Detach from any negative emotions that may arise. Breathe to release stress so you can sleep well. Breathe! Allow your soul to connect with God.

Binaural Beats

Listening to binaural beats with a pair of headphones or earbuds can benefit your mental health benefits and can promote clarity, focus, and concentration. It has also been known to help to reduce anxiety, lower stress and increase relaxation, foster positive moods and promote creativity, and help manage pain. It is excellent for use in meditation.

When you hear two tones — one in each ear — that are slightly different in frequency, your brain processes a beat at the difference of the frequencies. This is called a binaural beat. When listening to binaural beats, your brain gradually falls into synchrony with the difference.

HemiSync®, a leader in conscious media, was founded by Robert A. Monroe. Monroe achieved world-wide recognition as a ground-breaking visionary and explorer of human consciousness. His pioneering research, beginning in the 1950s, led to the discovery that specific sound patterns have identifiable, beneficial effects on our capabilities. For example, certain combinations of frequencies enhance alertness, others induce sleep, and still others evoke expanded states of consciousness.

"Assisted by a broad base of specialists in psychology, medicine, biochemistry, psychiatry, electrical engineering, physics, and education, Robert Monroe developed Hemi-Sync®, a low-cost, patented audio technology that facilitates enhanced performance.

"Using a Neuromapper, we can "see" hemispheric synchronization occur. Hemi-Sync® helps you safely alter your brain waves with multi-layered patterns of sound frequencies. When you hear these through stereo headphones or speakers, your brain responds by producing a third sound (called a binaural beat) that encourages the desired brain wave activity.

"A sound played in the left ear is heard as a single tone. A sound played in the right ear is also heard as a single tone. When played together the vibrato perceived is called binaural beating.[50]

HemiSync® has been helping people for more than fifty years. They have the largest online collection of content to help you relax, focus, meditate, sleep, and lead a more vibrant life. To learn more about HemiSync®, visit https://hemi-sync.com.

A Good Night's Sleep

A good night's sleep is important for optimal health. The amount of sleep a person needs depends on many factors, including age, vibration level, etc. People with a higher vibration need 5-6 hours per night, while the normal person needs 7-8 hours of sleep per night. The amount of sleep required also depends on whether or not a person has been sleep deprived. In other words, they may not get enough sleep one night and may have to make it up the next.

Too little sleep can cause memory problems, depression, an increase in one's perception of pain, and a weakening of the immune system. Too much sleep too often is a sign one is escaping life.

For a good night's rest, sleep with your head in the north and feet in the south. This way you are in the flow of life energetically. Make sure you have a good mattress and a good pillow.

Teeth grinding at night is a sign of too much stress. It can damage teeth and cause other oral health complications.

Too much stress can cause insomnia. Release stress by listening to soft, flowing music; e.g., Native American flute, classical, binaural beats, or nature sounds. White noise playing in the background can also help. Stay away from caffeine in the afternoon/evening if having trouble sleeping. Drink a cup of chamomile, lavender, lemon balm, passion flower, magnolia bark, and Valerian root tea at night for a better sleep.

---

[50] https://hemi-sync.com/

Sleeping in the fetal position is better because is allows the spine to rest in its natural alignment. Your brain does a better job of releasing when you sleep on your side.

Sleeping on one's back can cause snoring and/or sleep apnea as people get older. Shallow breathing or pauses in breath when sleeping is a sign of sleep apnea.

Restless leg syndrome is a sign a person's spirit legs are not in the physical legs. Crystal Surgery can put the spirit's legs back in the body. The results are immediate.

A Well-Rounded Life

As stated before, the key to a healthy, fulfilling life is balance in all areas and facets of your life. The secret to being healthy, wealthy, and wise is remembering to take time for you. "All work and no play" is not good for your personal or soul's growth.

As the saying goes, if you do not take time for you, no one else will. Take time for a stroll in the park, to smell the flowers, and to soak in the bathtub (using essential oils).

Pamper yourself! Go for a massage or facial, attend a yoga class, or experience reflexology. Go on a retreat. Feel good about yourself. Take time for a manicure or pedicure. Better yet, let someone else do it for you.

Take time for a game of golf or a day at the beach. Take time to laugh. Laughter is the best medicine. Laughter helps to release stress. It will prolong your life. During some part of your day, every day, find something to laugh about (no pretending!). If you don't have anything joyful or fun in your life, find it. This is critical! You must develop joy in some way, even a fraction of it every day—even in the midst of depression. Joy will help you to maintain light.

Take time for fun and relaxation, to laugh and to cry tears of joy, and to do something you enjoy. Take time to breathe. You are a beautiful soul! You are just as important as everyone else.

The Importance of an Alkaline Body

From a spiritual aspect, alkaline represents love and acid represents fear. A person with an alkaline body lives life from a place of love, while a person with an acidic body lives life from a place of fear. Fear eats away at the spirit body just as dis-ease eats away at the physical body.

What is pH?

pH stands for "potential Hydrogen," and it is a unit of measurement for the concentration of hydrogen ions in a solution. The pH scale is used "rank the relative basicity or acidity of substances to other substances, based on the amount of hydrogen ion activity in a substance."[51]

A measurement of how acidic or alkaline a solution is scored on a scale of 0 to 14.
- A pH of 0 to 6 is acidic.
- A pH of 7 is neutral.
- A pH of 8 or higher is basic, or alkaline.[52]

The optimal pH to maintain a healthy body is 7.4. A body that is acidic can lead to fatigue, headaches, chronic pain, lack of appetite, increased heart rate, depression, and more. Left unchecked, excess acid can lead to several more serious health problems, such as kidney stones, chronic kidney problems, kidney failure, bone disease, and delayed growth.[53]

---

[51] https://sciencetrends.com/what-does-ph-stand-for-and-mean/
[52] https://health.clevelandclinic.org/alkaline-diet
[53] https://www.developgoodhabits.com/how-to-make-your-body-more-alkaline/

Health Benefits of an Alkaline Body

The body stays strong when pH is maintained. Having a balanced pH protects our bodies from the inside out. Cancer cells cannot grow and dis-ease cannot exist in an alkaline body.

A body with a low pH or acidic body is low on minerals such as sodium, potassium, magnesium, and calcium. Minerals are important for the body to stay healthy because they keep our bones strong, muscles contracting, heart pumping, and brain working properly. They also regulate body processes and support the immune system.

An acidic body decreases the body's ability to repair damaged cells and detoxify heavy metals. It creates an environment for unhealthy organisms and tumors to grow, damages tissues and organs, and makes the body more susceptible to fatigue and dis-ease.

A balanced pH body, or alkaline body, supports overall immunity and disease resistance, maintains better detoxification and antioxidant protection, and can help neutralize free radicals and other harmful substances in the body.

Other health benefits of maintaining an alkaline body include:

- Slows osteoporosis and other bone diseases and improves metabolic acidosis by reducing bone loss
- Reduces the risk of cardiovascular issues, such as high blood pressure, heart attacks, and coronary heart disease
- Lowers the number of harmful bacteria within the digestive tract for better digestion
- Minimizes alkaline phosphatase (ALP) in the body and within the spine, which can lead to rheumatoid arthritis and brain tumors
- Relieves insomnia due to discomfort from chronic muscle or joint pain
- Reduces inflammation in the body which can lead to cancer and other dis-eases[54]

An alkaline body is one that has high energy levels and mental alertness. It can decrease stress levels and alleviate depression by elevating your mood. It is ideal because it supports oxygen delivery to

---

[54] https://www.healthfitnessrevolution.com/top-10-health-benefits-of-being-alkaline/

the cells to produce energy, promotes better digestion and metabolism function, contributes to an enhanced immune system, and avoids feelings of fatigue and lethargy.

An alkaline body can help to reduce the risk of cancer. A person with an alkaline body rarely gets sick, and if they do, it is usually due to a cold. A cold is the body's way to let you know it is run down and needs to be recharged. Over-the-counter medications mask symptoms. The ONLY cure for a cold is REST.

The Science Behind Body Alkalinity

Our bodies are constantly working to maintain a process known as homeostasis. According to Briticannica.com, homeostasis is "any self-regulating process by which biological systems tend to maintain stability while adjusting to conditions that are optimal for survival. If homeostasis is successful, life continues. If unsuccessful, disaster or death ensues. The stability attained is actually a dynamic equilibrium, in which continuous change occurs yet relatively uniform conditions prevail." [55]

One essential aspect of homeostasis is pH regulation. Homeostasis is maintained primarily by our kidneys and lungs. A healthy diet filled with fruits and vegetables, exercise, and proper sleep can play a significant role in maintaining a balanced pH in the body. It has been proven through research that an alkaline body may reduce the risk of certain chronic diseases while an overly acidic body (known as acidosis) can have serious health implications.

An alkaline body can be one of the most effective tools we have to enhance our overall health and well-being.

Test Your pH

There are only two root emotions in life: love and fear. Someone with an acidic body is living in a state of fear. Acid eats away at the body no different than fear. Someone with an alkaline body is living in

---

[55] https://www.britannica.com/science/homeostasis

a state of love. Fear is the absence, not the opposite, of love. Where love exists, fear cannot.

Test strips, also known as litmus paper, provide an inexpensive way to monitor pH levels. They can be purchased online. Most large pharmacies do not carry pH test strips.

To use the test strips, place a small amount of saliva or urine on the strip and wait for the color to change. Compare the pH color on the strip with the pH color on the chart to find your pH number.

Test your pH weekly with pH litmus strips. This is best done in the morning before you eat. Drink water or rinse your mouth to clear away old saliva from the night before, then use a test strip about 15 minutes after you have cleared your mouth.

Alkaline Diet

To achieve and maintain a balanced pH body, an alkaline diet is important. An alkaline diet consisting of a variety of fruits and vegetables reinforces healthy eating habits. Drink plenty of spring or mineral water, maintain a regular exercise routine, and cut back on sugar, alcohol, meat, and processed foods for even healthier results.

An alkaline diet can assist in keeping dis-ease away, increases your energy, and assists in losing weight. It can also reduce inflammation and infection in the body and helps to keep the body healthy to ward off unwanted viruses.

Fresh is best! One of the greatest benefits of eating fresh fruits and vegetables high in potassium, magnesium, calcium, bicarbonate, and herbs directly from the garden—whether it be your own garden or from a farmer's market—is that the nutrient-rich produce is at their peak flavor and nutritional value.

Alkaline-promoting foods include leafy green vegetables (spinach, kale, lettuce), root vegetables (beets, carrots, radishes), fruits (especially bananas, avocados, and citrus), nuts and seeds, and tofu. Consuming these foods can help balance the pH level in our body, thereby promoting better health and well-being.

Some foods, such as lemons and vinegar, can start out acidic but become alkaline-forming once in the body. Fish or lean meat can be acid-forming in the body, yet they are considered essential proteins vital for necessary for good health.

Cutting back on red meat (hooved animals), processed foods, alcohol and drugs (over-the-counter medications and pharmaceutical drugs) are also recommended for better results in creating an alkaline body.[56]

Stay away from processed foods as much as possible! When cooking a meal, you know what each recipe ingredient is and can easily obtain it. Now look at the labels of processed foods. Do you know what each ingredient/chemical/preservative is and how it can benefit the body? If you do not, you probably shouldn't be eating it. Food for thought...

Edgar Cayce was a clairvoyant, who aligned his mind with the universal consciousness and while in a trance-like state, channeled insights offering practical help and advice to answer questions asked by people from across the country. The majority of Edgar Cayce's readings dealt with holistic health and the treatment of illness. These insights or "readings" are still followed today, even though some readings are 100 years old.[57]

Edgar Cayce recommended a diet that is 80 percent alkaline to 20 percent acid. He also noted that because a food is acid is no indication that it remains acid in the body. It can turn to alkaline. Honey and raw sugars produce alkaline ash, but because of a high concentrate of sugar become acid-formers.[58]

Mediterranean Diet

The Mediterranean Diet is an excellent example of an alkaline diet. According to MediterraneanPlan.com, "The Mediterranean Diet is a way of eating based on the conventional cuisine of countries bordering the Mediterranean Sea. These include Italy, Greece, Spain, and Israel.

---

[56] https://www.mdanderson.org/publications/focused-on-health/the-alkaline-diet--what-you-need-to-know.h18-1592202.html

[57] https://edgarcayce.org/

[58] Edgar Cayce Readings © 1971, 1993-2007 by the Edgar Cayce Foundation. All rights reserved.

The diet typically consists of the region's conventional fruits, vegetables, beans, nuts, seafood, olive oil, and dairy—with perhaps a glass or two of red wine. The Mediterranean Diet is about more than just eating delicious, wholesome food though. Regular physical activity and sharing meals with family and friends are vital elements of The Mediterranean Diet. Together, they can have a profound impact on your mood and mental health and help you foster a deep appreciation for the pleasures of healthy eating and delicious foods. The Mediterranean Diet is an inexpensive and satisfying way to eat that can help you live a healthier and longer life." [59]

The human body requires a healthy balance of proteins, carbohydrates, lipids, vitamins, and mineral elements found in plants to obtain their nutrients for healthy growth and development. For example, carbohydrates found in plant foods (not processed foods) get converted into glucose, providing energy for the physical body.

God gave us everything we need to sustain life in a plant whether it is the food we eat or the remedy we take when we feel under the weather. The Mediterranean Diet is the best diet to follow for a healthier body and happier life.

Alkaline Water

Not all water is bottled equally. When purchasing alkaline water from a store, check the ingredients. If the first ingredient is purified water, it is not true alkaline water no matter what the label says. If the water is pure alkaline water, no additives should be included. Again, spring or mineral water are excellent choices for reasons stated earlier in this book.

Staying well-hydrated is critical to optimum health and well-being. Drinking plenty of alkaline (spring or mineral) water on a daily basis is

---

[59]
https://mediterraneanplan.com/quiz/?msclkid=4d07ff8011da130cce5b993e3f20c3d4&utm_source=bing&utm_medium=cpc&utm_campaign=Mediterranean%20Diet-USA-STATE-Ohio&utm_term=mediterranean%20diet&utm_content=Mediterranean%20Diet%20%5BMost%20Profitable%20Keywords%5D

critical to maintaining a balanced pH level. Alkaline water carries nutrients to cells, aids in digestion, flushes toxins from the body, and prevents dehydration. The best sources for alkaline water include:

Characteristics of Fiji Water

Fiji water is free-flowing, natural, filtered artesian water obtained from an aquifer in the Fiji Islands. The aquifer is a naturally occurring underground chamber that contains uncontaminated water. The pH level of unprocessed Fiji water is approximately 7.7, making it alkaline in nature. Fiji water:

- contains a higher mineral content to provide better circulation and improved skin health
- contains silica in higher amounts to build immunity and increased wound healing
- contains natural electrolytes
- helps grow longer, stronger hair and better nails
- helps in getting relief from headaches and migraines due to dehydration[60]

Fiji water is the best because "It begins as a cloud high above Fiji, over 1600 miles from the nearest continent. Slowly filtered by volcanic rock, it gathers minerals and electrolytes that create Fiji Water's soft, smooth taste. Earth's finest water. Bottled at the source, untouched by man. Until you unscrew the cap."[61]

Kangen Water®

Best used for drinking, hydration, and food preparation, Kangen Water® has a pH of 8.5-9.5. Electrolysis is the process that separates water into alkaline and acidic water. The pH level decides which water type that's being produced. With a Kangen® water unit, you can make your own healthy, alkaline, antioxidant drinking water that's rich in minerals and purged of impurities.

- Stronger acidic water (pH 2.7 and down)—for cleaning and sanitizing, commercial operation, and hygiene

---

[60] https://kidadl.com/facts/food-drink/facts-about-fiji-water-that-demonstrate-its-health-benefits
[61] https://www.fijiwater.com/the-water

- Beauty water (pH 5.5-6.0)—for skin and hair care, bath water, and pet care
- Clean water (pH 7.0)—for taking medication and preparing baby formula
- Kangen water (pH 8.5-9.5)—for drinking, hydration, and food preparation
- Strong Kangen water (pH 11.5 and up)—for cleaning food, food preparation, and stain removal

Purchase your own Kangen® antioxidant machine, rated the best machine on the market for home use, online or from a local distributor. For details, visit: https://www.kangen.com.[62]

John Ellis Water

John Ellis Water is structured water. When water is rapidly heated and cooled, it weakens the hydrogen bonds so it can easily be split into oxygen and hydrogen. By changing the bond angle in the water molecule of ordinary water from 104 degrees to 114 degrees (becoming structured water), people have been able to heal naturally as verified by oncologist reports.

John Ellis was the first person to figure out how to get rid of contagions, chemical diseases, and other pathogens from water which can cause serious or fatal diseases. Ellis owns 13 international patents that make nanoparticle free pure water (bacteria free) and his machines have passed 332 FDA tests. John Ellis Water changes the properties of water and cannot be duplicated by any other distillation system by any other water.

John Ellis Water has been proven to improve blood flow. Independent Blood Flow Studies and John Ellis Water have proven oxygen kills diseases and grows healthy bodies and even healthy fruits and vegetables when the hydrogen bond angle changes to 114 degrees instead of 104 degrees. "Since our blood is 94% water, the hydrogen molecule burns off the markers for anything you can name in your blood stream."

John Ellis Water will help you to feel amazingly healthy in a short amount of time. It is preventative maintenance, along with a healthy

---

[62] https://www.kangen.com/en_US/products#tabsd501p

diet, juicing, proper vitamins and supplements, exercise, prayer, and meditation.

The Link Between an Alkaline Body and Cancer

Studies have shown that cancer cells thrive in highly acidic environments. An alkaline diet can help to raise the body's pH levels, making your body a poor environment for cancer or any other dis-ease. It is a whole lot easier to *prevent* cancer than to release it once it shows up in the body.

We are fourfold beings. The mental, emotional, and spiritual bodies must be in balance, along with the physical body, to achieve and maintain an alkaline body.

Spiritually thinking, alkaline is symbolic of love and acid is symbolic of fear. All dis-ease is fear. Having faith and trust in God is love.

The Warburg Effect

Dr. Otto Heinrich Warburg, MD, PhD, was the son of a German physiologist and one of the world's leading scientists, studying chemistry under Nobel laureate Emil Fischer and later working with Albrecht Ludolf von Krehl, a renowned German internist and physiologist.

Dr. Warburg was appointed professor at the Kaiser Wilhelm Institute for Biology, where he began his research career. By 1931, he had become founding director of the Kaiser Wilhelm Institute for Cell Physiology in Berlin. He investigated the metabolism of tumors and the respiration of cells, particularly that of cancer cells. That same year, he was awarded the Nobel Prize for his discovery of a key respiratory enzyme, a protein which catalyzes a reaction necessary for cells to use oxygen.

Dr. Warburg was the first physician who theorized the cure for cancer with oxygen. In one of his medical reports, Dr. Warburg observed the lack of health that exists in every cancer condition had to do with impaired, oxygen-less respiration of the body's cells. He stated, "No disease, not even cancer cells, can survive in high blood oxygen."

Oxford University awarded Dr. Warburg a doctorate for proving "blood coursing through our veins, pushed by oxygen, kills the pathogens and diseases in our bodies." [63]

According to an article in the November 2010 issue of *Clinical Orthopedics and Related Research* (*Biographical Sketch: Otto Heinrich Warburg, PhD, MD*), Dr. Warburg was speaking to a group of other Nobel Laureates when he said, "Cancer, above all other diseases, has countless secondary causes. But, even for cancer, there is only one prime cause. To summarize in a few words, the prime cause of cancer is the replacement of the respiration of oxygen in normal body cells by a fermentation of sugar. All normal body cells meet their energy needs by respiration of oxygen, whereas cancer cells meet their energy needs in great part by fermentation.

"All normal body cells are thus obligate aerobes, whereas all cancer cells are partial anaerobes. From the standpoint of the physics and chemistry of life, this difference between normal and cancer cells is so great that one can scarcely picture a greater difference. Oxygen gas, the donor of energy in plants and animals is dethroned in the cancer cells and replaced by an energy yielding reaction of the lowest living forms, namely, a fermentation of glucose." [64]

Dr. Warburg proved cancerous tissues are acidic, whereas healthy tissues are alkaline. In his work, "The Metabolism of Tumours," he demonstrated that all forms of cancer are characterized by two basic conditions: acidosis and hypoxia (lack of oxygen). He discovered lack of oxygen and acidosis are two sides of the same coin: where you have one, you have the other. All normal cells have an absolute requirement for oxygen, but cancer cells can live without oxygen—a rule without exception. Deprive a cell of 35 percent of its oxygen for 48 hours, and it may become cancerous.

Before his death, Dr. Warburg was nominated for the Nobel Prize 47 times. He rejected all but the first one which awarded him a medical doctorate and lifetime residence in the Kaiser Wilhelm Institute. Otto

---

[63] https://johnellis.com/independent-blood-flow-studies
[64] https://doctorschierling.com/blog/why-everyone-should-know-who-dr-otto-warburg-was

Warburg's thesis proved that blood kills disease in the human body. The European medical community concluded Warburg was correct.

During his pre-laureate speech, Warburg said: "Nobody today can say that one does not know what the prime cause of cancer is. Ignorance is no longer an excuse for avoiding measures for prevention. How long [...a cancer cure]...will be avoided depends on how long the profit prophets succeed in inhibiting the application of cures based on scientific knowledge— not just in the cancer field, in diabetes, and even using serrapeptase to clear coronary arteries and veins in the eyes which will prevent blindness; and capillaries in the human fingers and feet in diabetics who need such minute veins and arteries opened to prevent the need to amputate fingers and toes. In the meantime, millions of men and women have unnecessarily died of cancer."

Conventional cancer therapies may prolong life, but they do not completely cure the disease. Patients using conventional cancer therapies will likely die much quicker than patients who consent to an oxygen-based treatment. Dr. Warburg believed the Food and Drug Administration, created by Franklin D. Roosevelt in 1933 and pressured by the cancer industry, banned all cancer treatments using oxygen. [65]

Sugar Feeds Cancer

Recognizing the important role of metabolism has led scientists to consider the role that increased consumption of glucose (a type of sugar) and glutamine (amino acids) plays in growing tumors.

In the book, *Ravenous*, Johns Hopkins faculty member Sam Apple explains how Dr. Otto Warburg's once disregarded cancer metabolism research has undergone a major resurgence.

According to Apple, metabolism-centered therapies have shown promise. Some researchers have focused on dietary cancer treatments such as feeding mice low-calorie diets or low-carbohydrate diets since carbohydrates break down to glucose. "These diets are not cures but have been shown to limit the growth of various cancers in

---

[65] https://johnellis.com/independent-blood-flow-studies

rodents," Apple says. "We still don't know if they are helpful for humans."

The book's final chapter highlights the much-debated role of Western diets as a significant contributor to cancer cases worldwide. According to Apple, understanding sugar and taking precautions to limit it in our diet have become analogous to tobacco and the long, drawn-out time it took for people to believe that smoking had deadly effects.

Dr. Warburg's pioneering work focused on how cells fueled their growth. In studying rat tumor cells in the lab, he found cancer cells ravenously consume enormous amounts of glucose compared to normal cells, which they break down without oxygen via fermentation. The discovery, later named the Warburg effect, is believed to be a hallmark of most cancers, including that in humans. In other words, Dr. Warburg figured out that blood sugar (glucose) is cancer's "meal of choice." [66]

Dr. Patrick Quillin is an internationally recognized expert in the area of nutrition and cancer. He has thirty years of experience as a clinical nutritionist, of which 10 years were spent as the Vice President of Nutrition for Cancer Treatment Centers of America where he worked with thousands of cancer patients in a hospital setting.

Dr. Quillin found: "In most major cancer hospitals around the world, oncologists use a $2 million device, called a PET scan (positron emission tomography), which detects cancer by finding hot spots of sugar feeding cells in the body. All of these world-class scientists are using the same principle: sugar feeds cancer. When we can lower blood glucose, we can slow cancer growth." [67]

He has also stated: "While chemotherapy and radiation can kill cancer cells, these therapies are general toxins against your body cells also. A well-nourished cancer patient can protect healthy cells against the toxic effects of chemo and radiation, thus making the cancer cells more vulnerable to the medicine. Proper nutrition can make chemo and radiation more of a selective toxin against the cancer and less damaging to the patient." [68]

---

[66] https://hub.jhu.edu/2021/06/04/ravenous-otto-warburg-sam-apple/
[67] https://beatingcancerwithnutrition.com/does-sugar-feed-cancer/
[68] https://beatingcancerwithnutrition.com/chemotherapy-nutrition/

Quite often. purified water, sodas, and processed sugar snacks (carbohydrates that eventually turn into sugar) are being passed out to cancer patients while receiving chemotherapy treatments when they should be given healthy food and drinks to boost the immune system.

How ironic! Patients are being given the very food that feeds cancer at the same time they are taking a poison to destroy cancer in their body. Does the medical establishment really want healthy patients? If they did, doctors would be preaching to their patients the importance of proper nutrition and a healthier lifestyle. The time for change is now.

Non-Conventional Cancer Treatments

With the sky-rocketing cost of medical treatments and pharmaceuticals, many patients today are looking for cost-effective, natural ways to improve health and maintain wellness. They seek healing through both Complementary and Alternative Medicine (CAM).

Despite all the wonderful advances in modern biotechnology and medical practices that have never been seen before, CAM has dramatically expanded and grown quickly over the past twenty years. Yet many conventional healthcare professionals refuse to take CAM seriously because "there is no research in CAM."

It is true there is a lack of scientific evidence today to confirm any type of natural healing. Why? Because the medical establishment has fought any natural method for healing, despite all the success stories of those who healed naturally.

Thousands of success stories exist of people who released cancer and lived after hearing an "incurable" diagnosis. This information is purposely being overlooked and suppressed by the people we rely on who have established themselves as "experts," yet the most interesting perspectives come from outside of the field.

There are natural cures for most, if not all, dis-eases (including cancer), but Big Pharma and their pocketed government officials will never allow natural cures to take root in this country. There is a lot of money to be made in pharmaceuticals. No one gets rich when nature is used to heal. Big Pharma and the medical profession need us all to not only get sick but stay sick in order to remain profitable. It is the sad truth of our times.

The largest healthcare organization in the United States, Kaiser, recommends a plant-based diet because it reverses dis-ease. People become healthier, experience less sick days, become more productive, and experience better moods. In other words, the healthier we are, the more money we will save.

Natural healing is not new! It has been around for thousands of years. Let's reeducate people and move forward into a place of good health and well-being by eating nutritiously and using Nature's remedies to heal.

Eastern Medicine vs. Western Medicine

Eastern medicine began in China over five thousand years ago and is still practiced today. It focuses on preventative health and natural healing. Western medicine traces its roots back to ancient Greek and Egyptian physicians, but it began to take the form as we know it today during the 19th century.

Eastern medicine takes into consideration the bigger picture. It examines all the "parts" of the body (mental, emotional, spiritual, physical) that make up the "whole." Western medicine looks at the "body" as an instrument that breaks down on its own. They do not look at all of the parts to understand why the body part broke down.

Eastern medicine believes everything is connected and that when everything is in balance, wellness is present. Dis-ease can occur when there is an imbalance in the mind, body, emotions, spirit, or environment.

Eastern medicine works to bring the mind, body, emotions, and environment into a state of balance. Natural herbal remedies, aromatherapy, breath work, movement exercises, and universal life energy are used to promote life and healing. These remedies work to strengthen the body's own defenses and help to restore balance to fight dis-ease. The more out of balance your body is, the slower the results will be. After all, it took time to create the dis-ease. It may take time to release it. The more ready someone is for change, the faster the healing.

Western medicine works to heal the injured body part and uses prescription drugs containing chemicals or unnatural substances to treat an illness. These drugs alter the brain chemistry, hormones, and/or mentality of the individual. They appear to work because they trick the brain into thinking something other than what we are experiencing. In other words, the brain does not send communication to the nerves, thus creating the feeling that everything is fine when it may not be.

104

When the body is in crisis, incapable of overcoming the dis-ease on its own, the Western method can be lifesaving and the best alternative. However, to prevent dis-ease and enhance regeneration, and to support the natural flow of energy to maintain wellness, the Eastern method has much to offer.

Each form of medicine has its advantages. Western medicine works to heal an already-injured or dis-eased part of the body while Eastern medicine works to prevent dis-ease by maintaining balance within the body. My advice is to recognize the symptoms, then work to heal them before dis-ease can settle into the physical body.

When a doctor cannot find an answer to a patient's symptoms, it may be because the dis-ease has not yet settled into the physical body. This is the best time to incorporate integrated healing—to release the symptoms *before* they settle into the physical body.

Bottom line: Eastern medicine is preventative while Western medicine is reactive.

Wholistic Therapies

Wholistic therapies are client-centered and incorporate the whole person, e.g., body, mind, emotions, and spirit. Many people who have an overage of cancer or another dis-ease are willing to try wholistic therapies to help them feel better after treatments and to assist them in their healing.

More than one therapy can be done at a time, and **there are little to no side effects with any of these treatments.** Effective ways to assist healing are through energy healing such as Reiki, sound healing, vibrational healing, and crystal healing. Art therapy, color therapy, music therapy, energy healing, sound healing, vibrational healing, and crystal healing are also effective therapies used in the treatment of dis-ease.

Wholistic therapies, such as those that follow, can help to relieve many symptoms associated with cancer or any other dis-ease.

Medical Disclaimer: Information and products shown are not to be used as medical advice and/or to be used in place of medical treatment of any kind. All information and products are to be used for educational purposes only. It is not a substitute for professional medical advice, diagnosis, or treatment. Always seek the advice of your physician or other qualified health providers with any questions you may have regarding a medical condition and before undertaking any diet, supplement, fitness, or other health program.

Acupuncture / Acupressure

Acupuncture is a conventional Chinese medicine that inserts tiny needles into the skin on strategic points at the body by a licensed practitioner. Do not use acupuncture when on blood thinners or if you have low blood counts.

Most commonly used to treat pain, it is progressively being used for overall wellness and stress management. It is a technique used to balance the flow of energy or life force (also known as chi or qi) through meridians in the body. Western practitioners also use acupuncture to stimulate nerves, muscles, and connective tissue in the body to boost the body's natural painkillers.

Acupuncture can also be used for chemotherapy-induced and postoperative nausea and vomiting, dental pain, fibromyalgia, headaches (tension and migraine), labor pain, back or neck pain, osteoarthritis, menstrual cramps, respiratory disorders (such as allergic rhinitis), myofascial pain syndrome, sciatica, chronic pelvic pain syndrome, irritable bowel syndrome, seasonal allergies, urinary incontinence, asthma, depression, quitting smoking, infertility, carpal tunnel syndrome, hot flashes associated with menopause, tennis elbow, and much more.[69]

While acupuncture and acupressure are rooted in the same belief (improving Qi by stimulating certain body points), the two are not the same. Acupuncture is a stronger therapy that can only be administered by a licensed professional. Acupressure requires pressure from the hands.

Relatively few complications from using acupuncture have been reported. However, complications have resulted from the use of nonsterile needles and improper delivery of treatments. Some health

---

[69] https://www.mayoclinic.org/tests-procedures/acupuncture/about/pac-20392763

insurance policies cover acupuncture, but others do not. Coverage is often limited based on the condition being treated.[70]

Aromatherapy / Essential Oils

Many essential oils are most effective; some are not meant for consistent use. WE set forth an understanding to some of you on the use of oils in healing early on in Earth's history. Now, first and foremost, intention in and with their use is everything. And the use, mixture, and creation of them is a science. Remember, from OUR last book, God and Science, One and the Same! Only the best sanctified and consecrated oils should be used, and you can sanctify and consecrate the oils yourself. The dietary relations of oils should be considered always and their effect on the human body as a whole. For all oils have some therapeutic value, some more than others. Therefore, be sure the oils you use are of a high therapeutic grade. It is important to ensure that no heavy concentrate of herbicides is present within the product. Sadly, everything on your planet has some herbicides within its makeup and composition, there is nothing you can do about that. All of you created such. Yet there are those with trace amounts and those are the ones that should be sought out. So, WE are telling you to, to the best of your ability, seek out the purest quality of oils that you can. ~ All There Is, Was, and Ever Shall Be through Elliott Eli Jackson[71]

Aromatherapy uses essential oils to stimulate and calm one's energy, sending impulses to the brain which control memory and emotion. The smell travels through the nerves inside the nose up to the part of the brain that controls our moods, memory, and learning ability. Oils are absorbed into the skin and blood stream to help alleviate a wide range of physical, mental, and emotional discomforts, including mood disorders, burns, infections, depression, insomnia, and high blood pressure. They can also assist in boosting the immune, respiratory, and circulatory systems. Aromatherapy has been found to be effective in relieving nausea, pain, and stress.

---

[70] https://www.forbes.com/health/wellness/acupuncture-vs-acupressure/
[71] The Sapiential Discourses Universal Wisdom Book III, by All There Is Was and Ever Shall Be through Elliott Eli Jackson

The use and blending of undiluted, pure essential oils extracted from specific aromatic plants can promote healing. Aromatherapy has been around for at least 6,000 years and been practiced by the Greeks, Romans, and ancient Egyptians. The Egyptian physician and teacher of Hippocrates, Imhotep, recommended fragrant oils for bathing, massage, and for embalming their dead. Imhotep used aromatic fumigations to rid Athens of the plague. More recently, in World War II, doctors on the battlefield would often use aromatherapy and herbal remedies as antiseptics on wounds.

Note: Use premium-grade essential oils for more effective results. Some essential oils applied to the skin can cause an allergic reaction.

Art Therapy

Art therapy incorporates drawing, painting, and sculpting to create well-being. Through art we can improve communication (especially people with mental or psychological disorders), release stress, and improve our social skills by helping to create a good self-image of who we are and what we can do.

Ayuerveda

The term 'Ayurveda' itself is derived from two Sanskrit root words: *Ayu* (life) and *Veda* (knowledge) or *Science* (Science of Life).

Ayurveda is one of the world's oldest holistic healing systems, originating over 5,000 years ago. It is a holistic science and looks at wellness as a whole. Perfect health is defined as a state of balance between mind, body, spirit, and social well-being.

Rather than treating just the symptoms, Ayurveda focuses on finding and treating the root cause of disease. Any type of disease is caused by an imbalance. Thousands of years of Ayurvedic wisdom and knowledge is well documented and can be found in ancient scriptures.

Every thought and practice in this system mirrors the dual principles of balance and connection. Ayurveda is best characterized as the science of living in tune with nature's laws. Ayurvedic philosophy of natural and holistic medicine encourages people to live a balanced existence by making healthy and natural lifestyle adjustments.

Ayurveda's knowledge is just as relevant more than ever today as it was in olden times.[72]

Binaural Beats

Binaural beats, according to The Enlightenment Journey, "are auditory illusions created when two slightly different frequencies are presented separately to each ear. The brain perceives a third tone, the binaural beat, between the two frequencies. These beats have the potential to influence brainwave activity, leading to various cognitive and emotional effects.

"Binaural beats are a type of brainwave entrainment technique that can alter your brain's electrical activity. They are commonly used for relaxation, meditation, stress reduction, improved focus, and even enhanced creativity.

"Some of the key benefits include: stress reduction and relaxation, improved focus and concentration, enhanced creativity and problem-solving skills, better sleep quality and insomnia relief, anxiety and depression management, mood regulation and emotional well-being.

Medical Disclaimer: If you have a history of epilepsy, seizures, or other neurological conditions, consult a healthcare provider before using binaural beats. Avoid listening to binaural beats at high volumes for extended periods to prevent hearing damage. Start with short listening sessions and gradually increase the duration to avoid any adverse effects.[73]

Biofeedback Consciousness

The QXCI/SCIO biofeedback consciousness is a non-intrusive extraordinary healing device. QXCI stands for Quantum Xeroid Consciousness Interface or "Quantum Med System," and SCIO stands for Scientific Consciousness Interface Operation,

The device or consciousness is non-intrusive and quantum in nature. "It measures electrophysiologically over 8,500 portions or functions of the human body, which is then translated by computer for diagnostic and therapeutic outcomes. It measures change, potential or

---

[72] https://theayurvedaexperience.com/pages/what-is-ayurveda
[73] https://theenlightenmentjourney.com/understanding-binaural-beats-a-beginners-guide/

otherwise, in brain waves, Galvanic Skin Response (GSR), skin temperature, and moisture. The device/consciousness then sends or transmits the appropriate frequencies to where they need to go within the body to assist the body in healing itself." [74]

This system was designed using the principles of quantum physics. A treatment with this device can be customized to treat general health or address specific concerns of the patient. The device scans the body looking for everything from viruses, deficiencies, weaknesses, allergies, and abnormalities. It reports on the biological reactivity and resonance in the body and resonance in the body and indicates needs, dysfunctions, and vulnerabilities.

This device balances subtle energies, allowing the body to heal itself. The trivector system measures the voltage, amperage, resistance, frequencies, etc. to calculate the inductance, capacitance, resonance and conductance of the reactive system of the body over time.

By adapting the work of Becker, Priori, Beardall and others, Professor Bill Nelson has developed a computerized system that can develop a tiny DC potential multi-signal to time reverse cells, using techniques such as differentiation and redifferentiation into a massive set of multi signal fractals. The non-linear analysis can then develop multi-signals for deep tissue interface. This can be used to stimulate immune function, destroy pathogens, detoxify free radicals, and others.

The Biofeedback Consciousness system has been used to help resolve problems like cancer and Parkinson's, infection and inflammation, fungus and molds, bacteria and viruses, anti-aging and rejuvenation, to name a few.

Medical Disclaimer: This device is designed for use as Biofeedback and Transcutaneous (on the skin) Electro Nerval Stimulation (TENS). The definition of Biofeedback is "measuring a physiological response and feeding it back to the patient." This system measures evoked potential reactions of the patient to applied stimulations. This is evoked potential Biofeedback. This device catalogs and tabulates the complex evoked potential Electro Physiological Reactions (EPR) of the patient.

---

[74] *The Sapiential Discourses Universal Wisdom Book III*, by All There Is Was and Ever Shall Be through Elliott Eli Jackson, pp. 100-101.

This is the EPR pattern. The accuracy of the EPR pattern is limited and, as such, the results cannot be treated as completely diagnostic. This device is not diagnostic, the readings are meant as prediagnostic. The doctor or practitioner should then use this data wisely and challenge the results with more standard medical measures, some of which are found in the disease dictionary. This device is safe and is of no risk to the patient. The potential benefits are quite amazing.[75]

Cranial Sacral Therapy

Cranial sacral therapy works with the cranial bones in the head, the spinal column, and the sacrum to balance energy, as well as the flow of cranial sacral fluid. This therapy is gentle enough to be used on infants, children, and the elderly. It has been used to help treat headaches, insomnia, sinus pressure, earaches, temporomandibular joint dysfunction (TMJ), and chronic pain conditions such as fibromyalgia.

Crystal Healing

Crystals have been used to assist in the healing process for thousands of years. They have been mentioned in the Bible. The high priest Aaron used them in his breastplate to communicate with angels. King Solomon's ring (gemstone) gave him power over the elements.

Throughout history, precious and semi-precious stones (crystals) were used in the crowns of kings and queens and in the statues of gods and goddesses, symbolizing their association with mystical powers. The diamond is used in wedding bands today as a symbol of purity.

Crystals are energy transmitters. They can absorb, focus, and transmit subtle electromagnetic energy. For this reason, they make excellent healing tools. Because crystals have a pure energy that vibrates at a fixed, stable, and unchangeable frequency, they can bring our energy level to its energy level. Upon coming into contact with a crystal, the vibrations of the crystal will interact with and change your vibration, matching your vibration with its vibration.

Crystals are used today in clocks, radios, microwaves, computers, and much more. There was resurgence in the use of crystals in the

---

[75] http://healingacademy.com/qxci/

1980s and 1990s. Interest in crystals grew and made headlines in newspapers, magazines, and television shows.

The human body cannot exist without minerals. The physical body can receive minerals from specific crystals by placing the crystal on the body.

Resonance is the key principal of crystal healing. Since most matter is crystalline in nature, our bodies take on the energy being transmitted from the crystal. Quartz crystals have a similar molecular structure to water, which responds when charged with crystal energy by developing a more coherent crystalline structure. Since our bodies are mostly water, healing intentions directed and amplified through crystals can easily transfer to our bodies and stabilize our health.

Crystals can be used in many ways: for healing, meditation, protection, and manifestation, to name a few. They can be used as an elixir and to improve the health of plants and an aura.

Crystal Singing Bowls (Quartz)

These crystal healing tools have been set forth in the Gadius Universal Atomic and Subatomic Blueprint or Plan to resonate with the chakra systems of the encasements on Earth. The tones produced by crystals not only are heard by the ear but are also transformed into missiles that seek out and penetrate areas of dis-ease and discomfort within your body. With the setting of certain tones is the ability to bring about healing, balancing equilibrium, and can be effective in extending and enhancing the meditation process. ~ All There Is, Was, and Ever Shall Be through Elliott Eli Jackson[76]

When a person's healthy resonant frequency is out of balance, physical and emotional health is affected. Science has proven energy is made up of vibration and frequency. Sound is heard not only in the ears, but in every cell of our body.

Sound healing is based on scientific principles. All matter, including the cells of your body, vibrate to a specific frequency when healthy and a dissonant frequency when dis-ease is present. Rhythms and tones have been proven to balance brain hemispheres, thereby

---

[76] *The Sapiential Discourses Universal Wisdom Book III*, by All There Is Was and Ever Shall Be through Elliott Eli Jackson, pp. 96-97.

reducing stress levels and tension in cells that have fallen into dis-ease or dis-harmony. Even bones and organs feel the tone and intensity of sounds and react accordingly.

Advocates maintain that sound therapy is effective in treating conditions such as stress, anxiety, high blood pressure, depression, and autism. They are effective in assisting spinal energy flow and strengthening the skeletal frame.

Crystal Surgery

Crystal Surgery is a form of crystal healing channeled in the 1990's by Vivien Schapera, a teacher and healer for over thirty years. Vivien teaches how crystals can heal the body, mind, and spirit, the chakras, energy field and energy body, and healing states of consciousness.

Crystals are used in Crystal Surgery as tools for "operating" on both the energy field and the energy body. Through systematic, direct changes in these two systems, indirect changes are stimulated in the physical body. Crystals are used like scalpels and other surgical instruments for scraping, cutting, cleaning, suctioning, and stitching. They simultaneously adjust wavelength and chemistry. Over time, crystal surgeons develop their own techniques, adding to the knowledge already learned.

Crystal Surgery has been used to clear negative energy, slow down/balance brain waves due to stress, release inflammation, relieve congestion caused by colds/sinus/flu, loosen joints to relieve pain, unbind the heart, heal past-life wounds, promote tissue regeneration, and much more.

Gong Baths

Gongs were designed to calm the mind. Their tones are set to affect the mental portion of human and animal brains, directly pinpointing the areas that deal with pleasure. Thus, the gong's tones have a connection to dopamine and the electrical impulses that are sent from them to the entire human body. These tones are able to send out or away lower trace portions of US/the universe that should not be in certain areas of the human encasement. Because gongs are suspended, their sounds and vibrations can go into all areas without any impediment from the ground. Additionally, gongs concern themselves with the organs of the

human encasement, for they are literally suspended within the body.
The tones and sounds of gongs have healing effects on the endocrine
system.[77]

The resonance of the gong helps shift the molecular structure of the room and those in it by setting up layers of vibrations in the air that resound through our emotional, psychological, physical, and spiritual bodies. The vibrations emanating from the gong move through all of the tissues and organs in the body, releasing blockages, restoring homeostasis, and creating a profound sense of peace and relaxation, bringing about balance and inner harmony.

Because gongs are suspended, their sound and vibration can go into all areas without any impediment from the ground, similar to that of the organs suspended within the human body. The tones and sounds of gongs create healing effects on the endocrine system and thyroid, also allowing for weight loss connected to the thyroid's function.

Gongs send out two distinctive sounds or vibrations that send out shockwave vibrations set between one to five Hz. Their pulse is violent, yet subtle enough to produce a healing effect on the body. Chanting, in connection with the gong, can project the sound of the gong to certain portions of the human being to create a subconscious, subatomic result.

Together, the use of crystal singing bowls and gongs create a harmonic overtone to stimulate all areas of the human body.

Hyperbaric Oxygen Therapy
According to Genesis Hyperbarics Health & Wellness Center in Middetown, Ohio, "Hyperbaric oxygen therapy is the process of breathing oxygen in atmospheric pressure greater than sea level. When oxygen is taken in at a greater pressure, the body is able to absorb it at much greater levels than if taken in at sea level. Greater absorption means the oxygen can be forced into the blood plasma, cerebral spinal fluid (the fluid that surrounds the brain and spinal column), bone tissue, and lymph nodes. The pressure also causes an increase in circulation throughout the body that can reach areas of blocked circulation even to

---

[77] *The Sapiential Discourses Universal Wisdom Book III*, by All There Is Was and Ever Shall Be through Elliott Eli Jackson, pp. 97-98

the point of growing new blood vessels to provide extra oxygen to compromised areas of the body.

"Hyperbaric oxygen therapy (HBOT) is a medical treatment, which enhances the body's natural healing process by inhalation of 100% oxygen in a chamber where atmospheric pressure is increased and controlled.

"Oxygen is transported throughout the body only by red blood cells. Oxygen is dissolved into all of the body's fluids, the plasma, the lymphatic system, the central nervous system fluids, and the bone.

"Oxygen can be carried to areas where circulation is diminished or blocked. In this way, extra oxygen can reach the damaged tissues helping the body to support its own healing process. The increased oxygen enhances the ability of white blood cells to kill bacteria, reduces swelling and allows new blood vessels to grow more rapidly into the affected areas.

- Provides a decrease in inflammation
- Mobilizes and migrates stem cells to areas of injury
- Maximizes the efficiency of wound healing at every stage
- Optimizes and potentially re-vitalizes cells not functioning at maximal capacity

"It has long been known that healing many areas of the body cannot take place without appropriate oxygen levels in the tissue. In many cases, such as circulatory problems and non-healing wounds, adequate oxygen cannot easily reach the damaged area. Hyperbaric Oxygen Therapy can provide the extra oxygen with minimal side effects. Hyperbaric oxygen therapy may improve the quality of life of the patient in many areas. Many conditions such as PTSD and stroke have responded favorably to hyperbaric treatment.

"In each session, the patient enters an oxygen chamber, where the air pressure increases slowly. Patients can often watch TV and feel no differently than if they were in a normal pressure environment. The idea is to increase the amount of oxygen in the body's tissues and red blood cells. The process can change the way the body heals." [78]

---

[78] https://www.genesishyperbarics.com/hyperbaric-oxygen-therapy

Hypnotherapy

Hypnotherapy, commonly known as hypnosis, is a trance-like state of elevated awareness where one can experience focused attention and heightened suggestibility that can help manifest our heart's desires. It is a simple, yet powerful process to eliminate negativity, release old limiting beliefs, and replace them with solid, powerful beliefs. Hypnosis has been proven to have many benefits, especially in the reduction of chronic pain, depression, anxiety, and eating disorders. It has been used to help people who desire changes in behavior, such as to stop smoking, lose weight, memory recall, and release addictive behaviors. It has even been found to be beneficial in helping people to release self-sabotaging behaviors that keep us from achieving success by reinforcing the belief that we are confident, creative, magnetic, wealthy, and deserving of all good things in life.

Hypnosis may be helpful for people who are experiencing anxiety, pain, and stress. It may also help prevent anticipatory nausea and vomiting that can occur if chemotherapy has made you sick in the past. Be sure to tell your therapist if you have a history of mental illness.

Infrared Sauna/Saunas

People have been using saunas for centuries. There are no reports of negative effects, beyond the cautions about any sauna experience. These may include the possibilities of overheating, dehydrating, and interference with medication, as well as the potential dangers for those who are pregnant, have heart disease, or are under the influence of drugs or alcohol.

Benefits include improved heart health, soothing sore muscles, pain relief, relaxation, better sleep, and aids in pushing away illness.[79]

Integrated Energy Therapy (IET)

Integrated Energy Therapy (IET), a form of energy healing, helps to clear cellular memory stored in our tissues that can affect our everyday life. It clears energy blocks by releasing the imprint causing the block, then fills in the affected area with light and love.

---

[79] https://health.clevelandclinic.org/infrared-sauna-benefits

Ionic Foot Detox

The Ionic Foot Detoxification system benefits all of the body's organs, including the liver, intestines, kidneys, lungs, skin, and immune system. It allows the body to become energized and stimulated to function optimally. It can help to rid the body of heavy metals, chemotherapy, excess medications, toxins from smoking, and more. When using the Ionic Foot Detoxification system, the body can rid itself of these toxins through its normal processes of urination, defecation, and sweating. When the body is able to eliminate toxins and metabolic waste, then inflammation, edema, and swelling all decrease, allowing the body to repair itself and reduce pain within muscles and joints.

The purpose of this type of foot bath detoxification process is to cleanse your body. Ions generated by the ion cleanse appear to travel through the body, attaching themselves to many different toxic substances, neutralizing them, and drawing them out through the feet. The toxic substances ionic foot cleansing removes are a result of a poor diet and high stress.

A body tends to accumulate these toxins over time, weighing us down and causing emotional and physical problems. Ionic foot cleansing is said to be essential in order to maintain health and high energy levels, avoiding disease, and providing long-term wellness.

The Ionic foot detox is practical for most people because there is no preparation of special meals, no disruption in routine, and no discipline required unlike many herbal or fasting remedies commonly used to achieve the same goal of detoxification and cleansing of the body. You can just sit back and relax as you soak your feet and let your body detoxify.

Life Coaching/Wellness Advocacy

A life coach / wellness advocate can give you keys to maintain self-empowered wholeness so your mind can feel peacefully directed. By removing emotional, mental and spiritual obstacles energetically, you can connect into greater self-confidence with your inner source of well-being.

Mandalas

The word "mandala" means "circle" in Sanskrit. Mandalas have been used throughout history in Atlantis, Lemuria, and all other ancient civilizations on Earth. They were used as a healing tool to synchronize one's being with the rest of the universe.

Mandalas are infused with sound and vibration particles. Drawn, colored, or viewed, they send out a vibration that affects the mental portion of our being, our brain, bringing about a calming effect. They affect our conscious and unconscious reality, causing us to raise our vibration. They can accelerate brain activity and stimulate the cellular memory on all parts of the physical body.

Mandalas are excellent tools for hyperactivity or autism. Autistic people are already at a very high vibration. They chose to come at this time to assist humanity in learning tolerance, patience, and compassion.[80]

Massage

Massage can relieve muscle tension and stress and promote relaxation. It can be light and gentle, or it can be deep with more pressure. Studies have shown that massage can be helpful in relieving pain in people with cancer. It can also help relieve anxiety, fatigue, and stress.

Always be sure to work with a knowledgeable massage therapist who regularly works with people who have cancer. Do not have a massage if blood counts are very low. Ask the massage therapist to avoid massaging near surgical scars, radiation treatment areas, or tumors. If you have cancer in your bones or other bone diseases, such as osteoporosis, ask the massage therapist to use light pressure, rather than deep massage.

Meditation

Meditation can help people with an overage of cancer by relieving anxiety and stress and improving mood. Meditate for ten to fifteen

---

[80] *The Sapiential Discourses Universal Wisdom Book III*, by All There Is Was and Ever Shall be through Elliott Eli Jackson, pp. 99-100.

minutes once or twice a day or take a class with an instructor. Better yet, meditate in a Salt Cave for an even greater experience!

Movement Exercises

Movement exercises, such as Tai Chi, QiGong, and Yoga help lower blood pressure and reduce insomnia. They help lessen chronic pain while at the same time improving mobility, flexibility, and strength. They may help relieve fatigue and stress and help you sleep better at night.

If you are new to exercising, start slowly and build your routine. The ideal exercise amount would be 30-60 minutes of exercise, three times a week. Many studies now show that a consistent exercise routine may help promote longevity and improve overall quality of life.

Music and Sound Healing

Sound healing has been used to treat conditions such as autism, depression, dementia and Alzheimer's in clients, including seniors and children. It is an effective way to relieve stress and anxiety and to bring about harmony. Sound healing includes listening to music, playing a musical instrument, or writing songs. Research has shown that listening to music has a positive effect on a person's heart rate, blood pressure, respiratory rate, and overall positive outlook on life.

Native American Sweat Lodge

The heat and steam of a sweat lodge can help cleanse the body and mind. It can rid the body of impurities, improve circulation, relieve joint and muscle pain, and help with respiratory issues. The heat can stimulate the immune system to combat illness and dis-ease.

According to Native Tribe Info, "The Sweat Lodge ceremony is a sacred ritual that has played an integral role in Native American culture for thousands of years. It serves as a way to connect with nature, honor ancestors, preserve culture, and connect with the spiritual world. Participating in a sweat lodge ceremony can provide participants with a sense of community, purpose, and peace." [81]

---

[81] https://nativetribe.info/the-sacred-sweat-lodge-a-vital-native-american-tradition/

Past-Life Regression

Past-life regression is the journeying into one's past lives while in an altered state to help a person to view experiences from past lives. Past life regression may help us learn about factors in relationships that are affecting us today or health problems that seem to have no basis in this life.

The goal of past life regression is to provide an understanding of the soul's memory in order to release, forgive, and grow spiritually. At any given time, you are the sum total of all your past lives. You are the beautiful soul you are today because of what you have learned—what to do and what not to do.

We live in a duality world. We came to Earth to experience all of the emotions, not just some of them. There is no right. There is no wrong. There is no good. There is no bad. There are only experiences from which we learn and grow.

Quantum Healing/Quantum Touch

Quantum healing is done or completed on a subatomic level. It is frequency driven and wave motivated and carried out. This kind of healing work involves looking through one's spiritual eyesight. You must be able to view the person or persons that you are working on internally. Quantum Touch does inner healing of the physical by assisting the body in rebalancing, refabricating, and reorganizing cells and energies within itself. And, as with all healing, you are assisting the person in healing themselves. The body naturally heals itself, so the healer, so to speak, is only as a sound technician overseeing the process with movement of waves and vibrations. Quantum Healing also assists in the outer healing of the body, all areas within and with on the 32-layer structure of the energy field can be affected during this process. By raising one's own vibration, one becomes connected to the Universal Energy Field that is, in essence, connected to every person, place, and thing within the universal structure of everything, everywhere. Then the healer is able to allow the flow of healing to come to and through them to assist your others. It is a most wonderful way to help your planet in its healing phase. ~ All There Is, Was, and Ever Shall Be through Elliott Eli Jackson [82]

Quantum Healing is similar to Reiki, yet different. Quantum Healing incorporates meditation, breathwork, and the placement of hands on certain areas of the body for healing to take place. Touch is important for without touch, we could accomplish nothing on Earth. During Quantum Healing, one can move atomic and subatomic matter within and if necessary, out of the human body. And it without a doubt works if one has an open mind!

Quantum Healing Hypnosis Therapy (QHHT®)

QHHT® is a powerful technique developed by Dolores Cannon in which an individual is induced to the Somnambulistic state of trance through visualization. Past lives are explored to gain a better understanding of the effect they have in the current life. Before the healing session is over, the Subconscious mind will answer questions the client may have regarding real life issues. Healing can also take place if the individual desires to be healed and if it does not interfere with the goals of the current life.

The Subconscious mind is a name Dolores gave to what others call the Higher Self or Consciousness. The only limitations are that of the imagination. Heal the past to heal the present.

Quantum Resonance Crystal Bed

The Quantum Resonance Crystal Bed melds science and spirit in gentle and effective ways that shift us from our old paradigms to new ways of being.

Bio-resonance Field: Our bodies are receivers and interpreters of vibrations. We have various organs that are designed to receive different types of vibrations. The eyes receive light, the ears sound, the hair touch or pressure, the skin temperature, the nose smell, and the heart receives magnetic and multidimensional energy. If our eyes were

---

[82] *The Sapiential Discourses Universal Wisdom Book III*, by All There Is Was and Ever Shall be through Elliott Eli Jackson, pp. 95.

readjusted so they could see what we hear, then the "sound" would have color.

The same holds true for the other sensors our bodies have. The sensory systems are designed to give us a broad spectrum of information through various mediums so we can use our bodies effectively. At any given moment, the human body can instantly report what is happening around us and in us.

When our bodies are performing sub optimally, they can sometimes be overwhelmed with vibrations that are not the highest. Moreover, when we have a self-limiting belief, then it will affect what we do with the vibrations in our field.

Vibration-Based Therapy: The crystal bed can create specific vibrations through light, sound, magnetics, etc., and do so in a way that relaxes the client and allows the intentions to flow. The special binaural beats created through the headphones will turn off the brain and stop the self-limiting beliefs for the time on the system. The vibrations generated throughout the massage table are carried into every cell in the body, allowing for the cells to feel the same resonance.

Specific frequencies are generated through the crystal holders, and the crystals are sending that information into the subtle energy body. Magnets and light are inside these holders. Because we are adjusting and resetting so many of the body's information systems, we can then have amazing results.

Homeostasis and well-being can occur in the body by allowing the natural organic flow of energy and information to infuse the cells and subtle bodies of the client.

The uplifting feelings after laying on the crystal bed typically last for days. When a client uses the system in a repetitive fashion (twice a week, one hour each visit) for four to six weeks, they will find lasting results. The reason for this is the replication of cells. As the cells in the body wear out and are replaced by new cells, they use the frequencies available for coding and information. When the cells have a consistently high vibration to work with, they will replicate with those frequencies in place.

Reflexology

Reflexology has been practiced for centuries. Pressure is applied to different points on the bottom of the feet (acupressure). According to Chinese medicine, there are different meridian points on the feet that correspond to different areas of the body. Studies have proven it can help with stress and relaxation, pain management, digestion, eye strain, and improved sleep. It can also be beneficial for diabetes.

Reiki

Healing can be sent from a distance to the past, present, and future self of a person. Remember, all time is now. Change can be caused in an entire bloodline, if necessary. It can be sent to our others on other planets and planes. It is a most wonderful spiritual tool. ~ All There Is, Was, and Ever Shall Be through Elliott Eli Jackson[83]

A Conventional Usui Reiki treatment feels like a wonderful glowing radiance that flows through you and surrounds you. Reiki heals as it flows through affected parts of the energy field and charging them with positive energy. It raises the vibratory level of the energy field in and around the physical body where the negative thoughts and feelings are connected. This causes the negative energy to break apart and fall away. The Japanese translation of Reiki is "Universal Life Force."

This 2,500-year-old Japanese healing art was rediscovered by Dr. Miko Usui in 1922. With Reiki, it is the power of love and universal life energy rather than our own energy that is being utilized. By simply placing our hands on ourselves or another, universal energy flows wherever it is most needed, thus restoring the body, mind, emotions, and spirit to its balanced state of wellness. Reiki is said to be beneficial for treating physical, emotional, spiritual, and mental dis-eases.

Reiki is a gentle, holistic, hands-on process that assists in physical, mental, emotional, and spiritual healing, is a simple, effective, and powerful method of natural healing. A treatment can replenish physical energy and help to restore mental and emotional clarity and focus.

---

[83] *The Sapiential Discourses Universal Wisdom Book III*," by All There Is Was ad Ever Shall Be through Elliott Eli Jackson, pp. 92-93

Reiki not only works to rid the body and mind of the symptoms of disease, it also treats the root cause. Reiki harmonizes and balances the body, resulting in a feeling of relaxation and well-being.

Reiki heals by flowing through the affected parts of the energy field and charging them with positive energy. It raises the vibratory level of the energy field in and around the physical body where the negative thoughts and feelings are attached. This causes the negative energy to break apart and fall away. In so doing, Reiki clears, straightens, and heals the energy pathways, thus allowing the life force to flow in a healthy and natural way.

Reiki works to improve the results of all medical treatments, acting to reduce negative side effects, shorten healing time, reduce or eliminate pain, reduce stress, and help create optimism. It can help reduce some of the side effects of drug therapy used after surgery and chemotherapy. In all cases, Reiki therapy supplies the body with extra life energy, enabling the body to bounce back more quickly from the burdens of surgery and chemicals.

The key to success is that the therapy be undertaken on a regular basis. When a person is enjoying good health, the regular therapy increases the body's built-in defenses which manifest as confidence and an outward harmony in dealing with everyday events. It bestows a greater ability to deal with stressful situations. A positive outlook on life will be gained. Once the blockages and toxins have been removed from the system, personal advancement and spiritual growth can be achieved.

Salt Cave Therapy

Salt naturally has detoxifying, antibacterial, anti-fungal, anti-viral, and anti-inflammatory properties that can contribute to the loosening of excessive mucus and improving the immune system. The healing properties of salt have been known through the ages, from the Dead Sea to the Himalayan salt mines. Even Hippocrates, the father of medicine, prescribed salt water for breathing ailments.

Salt therapy has been found to positively impact three primary health areas centering around the respiratory system, skin issues, and mental health concerns. The treatment is simple: sit, relax, and breathe.

Salt therapy has been found to have a positive effect on:

- respiratory issues such as colds, allergies, asthma, bronchitis, COPD, cystic fibrosis, emphysema, hay fever, rhinitis, sinusitis, smoking damage, and snoring
- skin conditions such as acne, dermatitis, eczema, and psoriasis
- mental health issues such as stress and anxiety, depression, insomnia, postpartum depression, Post Trauma Stress Disorder (PTSD), and Seasonal Affective Disorder (SAD)
- other issues such as Lyme disease

Salt crystals are an ideal source of negative ions. Negative ions are oxygen atoms charged with an extra electron. They are odorless, tasteless, and invisible molecules that we inhale in abundance in certain environments (near waterfalls, at the beach). Spending time in a Salt Cave is like spending time at the beach!

Soul Connecting/Soul Retrieval/Toning

Soul Connecting is a method to release negative emotions (i.e., pain, sorrow, anger, rage, sadness, grief, etc.) stored within the emotional body from current and past incarnations. Soul Connecting creates an opportunity for blocked emotions to be released, going back to the root wherever they started. Once released, a definite shift in well-being is experienced, bringing more peace into one's life.

A soul retrieval is then performed to call back those soul parts that left because of the trauma, followed by channeled toning, a form of sound healing, to break up negative energy blocks and to restore peace, balance, and harmony to the mind, body, emotions, and spirit.

Sound Frequency Resonant Healing

Healing and music have been linked together dating back to ancient Greece because different sound frequences have an ability to manipulate the human and altered consciousness.

The famous physician, philosopher, and mathematician Pythagoras was convinced that frequencies had a healing effect on the body and that daily exposure to music was beneficial for human health. Pythagoras was also responsible for discovering the harmonic relationships between mathematical ratios and different musical chords.

Mystics and musicians have been tapping into sound frequencies to inspire and motivate humanity for hundreds of years. Mind is the Master has shown sound healing benefits include:

- Stroke recovery therapy—Music therapy given to stroke victims has been shown to increase the speed of recovery of basic motor functions and speech.
- Hospital settings—Musical frequencies have been shown to reduce anxiety and promote higher morale in high-stress hospital and medical settings.
- Enhancement of acupuncture—Along with colored light therapy, the use of tuning forks in conjunction with acupuncture has been shown anecdotally to be more effective than the use of acupuncture alone.
- Cancer treatment without surgery—Scientists have only recently discovered that high-frequency noise can be used to attack and destroy cancer cells while eliminating the need for surgery that puts the patient at risk of post-surgical complications.
- Autistic sensory therapy—Some autistic children have been shown to react positively to sound therapy exposure.
- Brain wave entrainment—Touted among experts in alternative medicine as an effective way of treating a variety of ailments, brain wave entrainment involves exposing the brain to different sound frequencies to address a variety of cognitive issues from headaches and stress to premenstrual symptoms and chronic pain.
- Altering stress hormones—Musical frequencies have long been used for therapeutic purposes to calm people who are angry, frustrated, or stressed.
- Increased neurogenesis—Both in unborn infants and the elderly suffering from dementia, the use of healing frequencies and musical therapy have been used to promote neural health, reduce stress, and promote memory.
- Enhancement of physical rehabilitation programs—Those individuals who are undergoing physical rehabilitation

experience have been shown to experience improved results when exercising to a playlist of music that motivates them.

- Decreased pain perception—For those patients who have to deal with chronic pain issues, musical therapy has been associated with decreased pain perception and is an effective method for pain management that does not involve medication.[84]

In a 2011 Ted Talk at Skidmore College entitled, "Shattering Cancer with Resonant Frequencies," Anthony Holland talked about his findings. Holland is a music professor who has researched the effect resonant frequencies have on cancer and other microorganisms. He explained how frequencies can cause cells to vibrate and eventually shatter, no different than a high pitch can break a crystal glass. Once the resonance gets larger, the glass breaks.

Holland discovered the ability of Oscillating Pulsed Electronic Fields (OPEF) to destroy cancer cells and MRSA in laboratory experiments. In his Ted Talk, Holland spoke about how cancer is vulnerable between 100,000 Hz and 300,000 Hz. Specific microorganisms can be targeted with specific frequencies. It is these frequencies that can shrink and break up tumors and destroy cancer cells.

Holland demonstrated his experiments using a plasma antenna device to target leukemia, ovarian, and pancreatic cancer cells, as well as MRSA, an antibiotic-resistant bacteria.[85]

Today, sound frequency can be achieved through a variety of methods, such as binaural beats, singing bowls, tuning forks, drumming circles, and vibrational-acoustic therapies. It is a growing industry to assist in healing the fourfold body. Measurements can be taken to demonstrate the powerful effect music and sound therapies have on our minds and bodies.

---

[84] https://www.mindisthemaster.com/sound-frequency-healing-human-body-benefits/
[85] https://www.youtube.com/watch?v=DYM6q42VxzY

Wouldn't it be wonderful if this type of technology could be made available worldwide to provide a nonpoisonous, painless, natural form of treatment for healing cancer patients, especially children!

Touch for Health

Touch for Health has been safely used in over 100 countries since 1973. It works to balance posture, attitude, and life energy for greater comfort and vitality. It is "a synthesis of ancient knowledge of the Chinese acupuncture meridians and techniques derived from chiropractic, naturopathy, osteopathy, and even person-centered counseling, including acupressure, a variety of touch reflexes, meridian tracing, nutrition and a variety of mind-body techniques for balancing the subtle energies while focusing on meaningful, personal goals."

Muscle testing (kinesiology) is used to identify imbalances in the body's energy system. As the body's energies are rebalanced, the body's intrinsic healing process is activated so that the body can better heal itself more effectively and more rapidly.

Benefits include:

- Clear mental/emotional/physical and energetic blocks
- Increase energy and vitality and counteract fatigue
- Relieve pain and release tension—headaches, backaches, stomachaches, arm, shoulder, leg and knee pain
- Release mental and emotional stress and being overwhelmed
- Enhance health and wellness and help prevent disease and injury
- Accelerate recovery from illness and injuries
- Improve performance at work, school and at home, in sports and in relationships
- Identify foods which enhance your energy and foods that don't
- Balance your energy flow to enhance your personal bests, achieve more consistent and frequent peak performance, reach your life goals, and enjoy life to the fullest

Medical Disclaimer: The Touch for Health model does not diagnose or treat named diseases or focus on treating symptoms. It was designed to be complementary to appropriate professional health care. Touch for

128

Health encourages proactive and timely consultations with qualified healthcare professionals to determine if you have a medical condition, and whether balancing the posture, emotions & energy is appropriate for your condition. We rely on the individual being healthy enough to determine for themselves if TFH is beneficial and whether they need to seek expert care. For serious illness, injury, or continuing, worsening or severe symptoms, always seek the services of a health care professional. [86]

Tuning Forks

Tuning forks are acoustically designed to resonate a specific ongoing tone or pitch. They are pure tone. The information for them was received from US by John Shore, a musician, unknown to many, on a spiritual quest to find the perfect sound or sounds of the universes. Each fork can be set for notes and frequencies in hertz that are directly connected to the rotation and vibration of your planet. The sounds are frequencies that affect the entire human body. The octaves are set to bring about recalibration and rejuvenation to everything around the vibrational circumference of the sound that emanates from the striking of the forks. This means that, when they are used in healing work, any mass—physiological or inanimate—is synchronized. Tuning forks are very powerful in the healing work. ~ All There Is, Was, and Ever Shall Be through Elliott Eli Jackson[87]

The shape of the tuning fork allows the two tones that occur during striking to warp each other and create the appropriate vibration necessary for healing to take place. Tuning forks can assist in the releasing of cancer. Tuning forks are effective in sending away lower portions of the universes that are connected to depression and addiction.

Weighted tuning forks can be used on meridian points to produce effective results. The human body functions harmonically. Since sound affects us at both the conscious and unconscious levels, it has the effect

---

[86] https://www.touch4health.com/about-touch-for-health
[87] *The Sapiential Discourses Universal Wisdom Book III*, by All There Is Was and Ever Shall Be through Elliott Eli Jackson, pp. 98-99

of counterbalancing the physical and emotional states of the body and the mind. The internal and external can be brought back into harmony and flexibility through sound.

Tuning forks create resonance throughout the fourfold being. Strike a tuning fork and the tines begin to vibrate. The back-and-forth vibration of the tines produce disturbances of surround in air molecules and energetic blocks in the energy field and energy body. They can create deep levels of healing by bringing your energy body and energy field back to its fundamental Hz or resonance, reconnecting you to the flow of life.

Sound healing therapies have been proven to equalize brain waves, increase the depth of breathing, slow the heartbeat and pulse, lower blood pressure, reduce muscle tension, increase circulation and endorphin production, boost the immune system, improve memory and learning, increase endurance and productivity, strengthen digestion and decrease depression.

The Healing Journey

The healing journey is not an easy one. It requires introspection, looking at the self to see how change must manifest. The only thing we can count on in life is change. A large part of the healing journey is learning to embrace our light and our shadow side.

The following is an excerpt from *The Secret of Life Wellness* by Inna Segal. The words perfectly express what it means to embrace your light and your shadow.

"Our shadow side consists of aspects of ourselves that we are least familiar with—aspects that we bury, resist, and suppress. This is where we try to mask all our insecurities, fears, disappointments, and failures, as well as our potential greatness, influence, beauty, integrity, and uniqueness. We yearn to be accepted and acceptable. Often, our greatest fear is to be labeled as different, weird, or unusual. Thus, we try to detach ourselves from our deepest apprehension, that somehow we are unwanted, worthless, false, unlovable, shameful, guilty, or damaged.

"In order to escape from looking within and discovering our perceived darkness, we attempt to cover up, trying our hardest to either please others or to resist them. We also project unconscious aspects of ourselves onto others. This can include positive and negative characteristics or personality traits that we disown.

"We might want to understand that our shadow aspects are the keepers of our greatest power. Much of our authenticity, potential, greatness, creativity, success, passion, and contribution in life are concealed within our own self-imposed barricades.

"Since many of us are encouraged to strive for perfection, we lose sight that our true beauty, lovability, growth, and evolution arise from embracing and loving our imperfections, idiosyncrasies, and individuality.

"Our ability to fully love and accept ourselves and others is greatly hindered by our need to hide and deny our limiting patterns, emotions, and behaviors. Instead of allowing our highest aspects to lead, being comfortable with ourselves and showing others who we truly are, we hand over control of our lives to our fear, resentment, rejection, hurt, anger, and neediness, without the awareness that we are doing so. Few of us realize that our neediness can hold the gift of love and the desire to help others, just as anger can offer up passion and our selfishness can make us stop, rest, and take care of our needs.

"It's amazing how many of us are terrified to discover that we might be powerful, ingenious, and extraordinary as we are of finding out we are average, weak, or full. Our shadow aspects become dominant when we refuse to have empathy for our own and other people's challenges.

"The shadow can be viewed as painful, unprocessed parts of ourselves that have the potential to hinder many aspects of our lives at the most appropriate moments, or when we are least prepared. As our shadow aspects are often controlled by our subconscious mind, it is easy for them to permeate our daily life and wreak chaos without us being aware of how this is occurring.

"Our self-sabotage can manifest in subtle and potent ways when we arrive to places late, miss opportunities, become involved with questionable characters, misread things people say, destroy potentially empowering relationships, and so forth.

"When you disown your shadow, you embark on a journey of fear, guilt, anger, and separation. You stop listening to, or trusting, the combined wisdom of your mind, body, heart, and soul and begin the process of internal confusion and conflict.

"If you choose to solely follow your feelings, you can turn into an overemotional, needy, insecure, doubtful indecisive, and dependent person. If you allow the mind to rule, you can become judgmental, controlling, and overly analytical. You are likely to make decisions based on logic and what you know without taking feelings, intuition, and wisdom into consideration. If your spiritual aspects are given all the power, you can become impractical, dreamy, and unrealistic, lost in mystical fantasies and desires of being saved. The idea is to create a healthy, balanced relationship between your heart, mind, and spirit.

"As long as the mind, emotions, and soul feel split and lack the ability to communicate with each other, you will feel doubtful and unsure about what actions to take, how to connect to others, and how to live in harmony with yourself. Your shadow aspects can push you toward healing by motivating you to ask questions and embrace more of who you are.

"In order for you to become self-empowered, you need to move from living outside yourself to connecting to your body, intuition, and inner life. This requires bringing light to those shadow aspects that are entrenched in limiting patterns and helping them to mature.

"For example, you may be repressing the fact that you are not emotionally and energetically compatible with your partner. If you were honest, you would confront your partner and work together on changing your relationship, or you would choose to leave the relationship. This would require courage, trust, candor, and a lot of personal growth. However, if you were to keep suppressing the fact that your relationship is not working, because you are afraid of being alone, you might become negative and aggressive, lie, cheat, or cause destruction in your life, creating dis-ease just to be safe.

"A huge part of your healing journey is to confront your shadow aspect, take back your power—your life force energy—and expand your freedom and the choices available to you."

Fear Can Affect the Physical Body

The only thing that stops us in life is fear. We have more fears than we can imagine! If left unchecked, fear can show up as dis-ease in the body so show us what is going on within.

Fears come from unresolved traumas from the past or in a past life. Traumas can be big or small. When a fear comes up in your life, it is important to first look at the lack or loss within the fear. For example:

- Those who feel like they have no control in their life try to control and manipulate others.
- Those who are envious or jealous are afraid of losing something.
- Those who become greedy are afraid they will not have enough.

- Those who cannot move beyond poverty have low self-worth.
- Those who judge are afraid of being judged themselves.
- Those who always draw attention to themselves have a fear of not being important.
- Those who are afraid of being rejected have a fear that they are not good enough or are a failure in life.

We have 18-24 hours to release a trauma. If we do not release the trauma (let it go), we store it in a particular body part within the spirit body. Pain is held in the spirit body. When the body part gets full, the emotion will flow over and into the physical body as dis-ease to show us what is going on within. For example:

- Fear of the spoken or unspoken word (ears, mouth, throat)
- Using our thoughts (brain) and words (mouth, throat) in a negative manner
- Choosing not to speak up for what is right when we know we should (mouth, throat)
- Fear of speaking up for ourself (voice)
- Fear of moving forward in life (legs)
- Fear of making a major decision which affects the future (hips)
- Fear of not wanting to see (eyes)
- Fear of not wanting to hear something (ears)
- Fear of finding joy in life (blood)
- Fear of being wrong (bones)
- Fear of losing control (muscles)

Most of us live our lives from fear, not love. We think we are living our life from love, but it is a conditional love. It has restrictions. "I'll love you as long as I know you." "I'll love you as long as you don't hurt me." "I'll love you as long as I'm getting out of our relationship." Unconditional love has no restrictions.

If we cannot love ourselves, we cannot truly love another. Everyone in our life is an aspect of us. What we don't like in others, we don't like about ourselves.

How can we tell if we truly love ourselves? By the way we take care of our fourfold bodies. If you love your car, you take good care of it. This is no different than taking care of your body.

Forgiveness

True forgiveness comes from the heart. It frees the soul to move on. Words are easily spoken, but not always meant. Forgiveness is important so that you and others can be free of the past. Forgiveness is being free of the pain and suffering felt from the experience. Forgiveness is important so change can take place, so all parties can be at peace.

Accept responsibility for your role in the situation. Request forgiveness for whatever you may have contributed to the situation, intentionally or unintentionally, and extend forgiveness to whomever hurt you. And don't forget to forgive yourself for your lack of understanding.

Apologize for not accepting others for who they are and forgive yourself for not accepting yourself for who you are.

Ask forgiveness from the person you hurt. Accept responsibility for your mistake and work to resolve the situation. Forgiveness is a requirement if true and lasting change are desired.

Always Choose Love

Everything begins with a thought. Keep your thoughts positive and loving. When you change your way of thinking, you change your way of being. The only way to heal is by changing you. When you change, your world and your physical body will change with you.

For you to remain healed, inner peace must be maintained. The time has come to take responsibility for our own health, to be self-empowered. Poor health and dis-ease do not "just happen." They are there to show us what we need to change within us.

A Lifestyle Change

As long as you are getting something out of your illness, you will not heal. There are trade-offs with everything in life. Sometimes people hang onto an illness because the fear of dealing with a situation is worse than the pain of the illness itself. Believe it or not, some people use their illness to get attention or because they do not want to work. Other people have had their illness so long they have "become" their illness. They have lost sight of who they really were before they got sick. And sometimes illness is karmic. There are many reasons we hang onto illness.

An alkaline diet alone cannot prevent or release an overage of cancer in the body. For true healing to take place, a lifestyle change is required.

Miracles take place when people believe! In order for a "miracle" healing to take place, you must believe with all your being that all things are possible with God (or whatever name you choose to call the source of all energy). There can be no doubt—for the slightest bit of doubt, worry, or fear lessens or cancels the "miracle" taking place.

Stay positive and loving at all times, and the energy you give out will return to you in the form of good health and a long, happy life. Self-centeredness, negativity, and fear will return to you in the form of drama, illness, and a short, unhappy life. Clear thinking and a loving spirit are imperative to maintaining wellness. When the mind, body, emotions, and spirit are in a constant state of peace, dis-ease cannot enter the body. If the mind, body, emotions, and spirit are in disharmony, dis-ease will be created to teach a lesson.

For true healing to take place, the fourfold body must be maintained to achieve an alkaline body. Small, consistent changes in your lifestyle can substantially impact your balance, well-being, and overall health over time. Do what you can whenever you can. Give gratitude and recite decrees throughout the day. Whatever you do will make the difference between just surviving and thriving in life.

If you choose to use conventional medical therapies, follow this advice as well. It can only help. Miracles do happen. We see them happen quite often at White Dove Circle of Light and Love!

Watch Your Words!

At the root of every dis-ease is fear. FEAR (False Evidence Appearing Real) is the most destructive energy in the universe. The more we fear something, the more we draw it to us by creating the very circumstances we wish to avoid. Through fear, we can even create a condition or situation that was not written into our script to experience before we came into life.

Your life is created by your thoughts, beliefs, words, and actions. If you don't like what is happening, change your thoughts, beliefs, words, and actions. The more attention you give something, the faster you bring it into fruition. Our words validate what we are thinking. Listen to your words!

NEVER say "I have cancer" or you will continue to have it. You own it! If it were that easy to get rid of something we own, we would all have cleaner houses. Never "own" cancer or any other dis-ease, or you will have trouble releasing it. Instead say, "I Am releasing cancer" or "I had cancer." Put cancer behind you.

NEVER say "I am fighting cancer" or you will continue to fight it. You cannot release something you are fighting. Instead say, "I Am releasing cancer." As long as we need a dis-ease, it will be there for us. As long as we are talking about the dis-ease, we have not let go.

NEVER say "I am a survivor." It implies you believe you were a victim, and there are no victims in life—only co-creators of circumstances. In other words, you drew it to you, and you are the only person who can release it. No one else can or will do it for you. Instead say, "I Am a champion."

A strong faith can overcome any fear. It is possible to move mountains—the mountains we make out of molehills in life—and it is possible to release dis-ease by releasing the fear associated with the dis-ease. Knowing (no doubt) it will happen is much stronger than believing or will happen.

The body was designed to be "self" healing. That means it needs your assistance to achieve your desired health and well-being. If it is not your time to die, no matter what you do, you will not die. Learn the lesson of the dis-ease, then work to change you.

Look at Self

It is important to know your spirit body is identical to your physical body. It has within it every organ, muscle, nerve, blood vessel, bone, etc. Your spirit body resides within the physical body, like a hand in a glove.

Each body part holds a different emotion. For example, the heart holds love (love of self, love for others), the legs move us forward in life, and the liver holds extreme anger. The body part is a container within the spirit body that holds emotion. These emotions stay with us, lifetime after lifetime, until we are ready to release them, until we have resolved them.

When the container is full, it overflows into the physical body as dis-ease to show us what we are holding onto, as if to say, "You have way too much of this. There is no more room in here. Clean up the mess!"

Now that you understand more about your spirit body, it is time to look at what is taking place in the spirit body when there is an overage of a stored emotion. If you truly want change to take place, ask yourself a few questions.

In what part of the body is the overage of cancer showing up? This will give you more insight as to the overflowing emotion. For example, breast cancer is "mothering to the point of smothering." This person is a "people pleaser," sacrificing his or her wants and desires for someone else who will, over time, not appreciate what is being done for them because there is no balance. There are no boundaries. Boundaries with consequences must be learned and used.

Leukemia is a blood dis-ease. Joy is stored in the blood. Someone with leukemia is holding onto anger and resentment, which is taking

139

their joy of life away. Beliefs are stored in the bones. Blood is made in the bones, which means this person also has a belief system out of alignment.

On which side of the body is the overage of cancer? The left side of the body has to do with the past and past lives. The right side of the body has to do with the current time. Look for the timeframe here.

What happened right before the overage was found? What emotions were you experiencing? Ask your client these basic questions, and they usually know what it is.

The next step is to determine where the root of the emotion lies. Is it in the current life or in a past life? Ask the person to body or muscle test to determine where the root is. If the root is in a past life, a past-life regression is highly recommended. Like a weed, if you do not get to the root, it will return.

Three Steps in Healing

There are three steps that must be followed to achieve a true and lasting healing:

Acceptance is the first step in healing. Once we can accept what happened, we are ready to heal. If you drowned in a past life, you were busy fighting for your life, not accepting what was happening at the time. This unresolved trauma will present itself to be resolved in a later life.

Understanding is the second step in healing. Understand what happened, why it happened, how it happened. Look deep. What was your role in the situation? Was it something you did or said, or something that happened to you, possibly because of karma, or was it something you chose to experience. How could the situation been handled differently? What lessons were learned? So many questions to ask!

Releasing is the third step in healing. ALL true healing is releasing. Release the trauma by writing a gut-wrenching, tear jerking, heartfelt release letter. When you are through, read the letter out loud to get the last of the emotion out. Tear up the letter (represents the soul contract between the two people) up. Burn the letter in a fireproof pan or abalone shell (represents the purification taking place within you), making sure you get every last piece burnt. Like a weed, you don't want to leave anything left behind to reappear.

Now say a prayer to God, asking to resolve the situation, then throw the ashes to the wind (the final release). Make sure the ashes go with the wind, not back at you. If the ashes fly back at you, it means you haven't released everything.

You may notice the wind may pick up when you go to burn the letter. This is a good thing! The winds represent change. It means change is taking place within you. If any anger and resentment come up unexpectedly, write another release letter. There was more to release. Sometimes we may have to write several letters before our emotions are completely released.

Prepare for Change

Now that the release letter(s) has been written, it's time to get ready for change. The time this takes varies from person to person, depending on how aggressive the cancer is and how determined the person is to bring about change, to heal.

The fourfold body must be brought back into balance. An alkaline body must be achieved and maintained. Remember, no dis-ease (not even cancer) or virus (not even the flu) can exist in an oxygen-rich, alkaline body.

The recommendations that follow are not difficult and will balance your fourfold body—proof you are on the path to healing.

The suggestions may seem a little overwhelming at first, but it's really not too bad. Make it a daily routine so it can become a positive behavior pattern to get you healthy and staying healthy. The only one who can do this is you. You have a choice: do the work or not do the work. Are you ready for change? If so, do the work!

Healing Through Belief

Gregg Braden, MD, best-selling author and 2020 Templeton Prize Nominee, is renowned as a biologist, visionary, scholar, and pioneer in the emerging paradigm based in science, social policy, and human potential. Gregg often talks about how quickly our beliefs can change our reality.

In one of his videos, he talks about how it has been proven, with video documentation from medicine-less hospitals in Beijing, China, that it is possible to look into the body of a living woman with a cancerous tumor Western science had deemed inoperable and watch the tumor break up and disappear as three practitioners, who understand the language of human emotion, see this person as whole, healthy, vital, completely enabled, and completely capacitated.

If the belief is strong enough among themselves, these practitioners can change the women's physical body as it mirrors their feeling. This can be watched through sonograms where the tumor disappears in less than three minutes. That's how quickly reality can change![88]

Change your beliefs to change your way of being, your world, and your body. Everything begins with a thought, but a thought goes nowhere without a belief. The more we believe something to be true, the faster we bring it into reality.

---

[88] https://x.com/BarbaraOneillAU/status/1811558075662221823

A Recipe for Change

Your body is your lifelong companion. Taking care of it is one of the greatest investments you can make for a healthy, happy life. Here are some things you can do to bring your physical bodies into alignment.

Get up a little earlier than you usually do. Begin your day with a new routine and a new attitude. Believe and have faith with every part of your being that what you are doing is working for you. With faith, we have everything. Without faith, we have nothing.

The most important thing that you can do to heal is to release fear. The more you fear something you don't want, the more you create it. Focus on what you want, not what you don't want. Create an alkaline body. Heal the mind, emotions, and spirit so the physical body can heal.

Here are some things to help dispel fear and create true healing in the body. Remember, cancer does not have to be a death sentence. It is a "wake up" call to show you what is going on within you. Change you, and your world and physical body will change with you!

Say out loud every day: "I Am sending all remnants of cancer from my being other than those naturally assigned. I Am shrinking any masses or tumors." Repeat this statement five more times throughout the day and once more at bedtime, for a total of seven times. *This is most important! Try not to miss a day.*

Begin Your Day

Set your intention to release all cancer and dis-ease from your body by decreeing out loud:

"I Am beautiful! I Am beautiful! I Am beautiful! And I Am ready for a wonderful day! I Am ready to give all that I can give and receive all that I can. I Am healed, dear God, because of your love. Thank you."

Breathe! Breathe in God for God is in the very air that we breathe. Take three to four nice deep cleansing breaths, in through the nose, out through the mouth.

Spend time in prayer. Say your prayers out loud, if possible, so they can be heard by the Universe. Everything is sound and vibration. Thoughts are vibration. When you add sound to a thought, a powerful combination is created to attract what you desire.

Give gratitude for what you want more of in life. Give gratitude for the releasing of all unnecessary cancer from your entire being, for healing, for perfect health and well-being, and more. The more you give gratitude for something, the more you receive of it.

Meditate for at least ten minutes, eyes open, back straight. The purpose of meditation is to align the fourfold body. At first, as you sit silently trying to clear your mind, you will be flooded with random thoughts. To quiet the mind, watch a moving object. The movement of the object will help move the thoughts out and slow down the mind, reaching a still point of peace and harmony within you. Allow the thoughts to come in. Be the silent witness. Decide which thoughts to keep and which to release. If you are reminded of a distant or recent situation that was painful, look at it from a different perspective. Get rid of the nonsensical thoughts that run through your mind so you can bring in new, insightful thoughts. If new information is received, write it down rather than trying to remember it.

Recite the *I Am Decrees*, *Books 1 and 2,* as given to us from All There Is, Was, and Ever Shall Be. These books are available for purchase on Amazon, in White Dove Circle's Gift Shop, or by visiting www.whitedovecircle.org.

Eat a healthy breakfast and take the appropriate vitamins and supplements to support your diet, being sure to include vitamin C. The ground is not as rich in minerals as it was hundreds of years ago. Because of this, everyone should be taking at least a multi-vitamin daily to maintain a balanced pH level. Zinc and a good brand of fish oil will help with hair loss. Body test or muscle test to see if there are any other vitamins, minerals, and supplements your body needs. Check for the proper dosage, time of day to be taken, and brand of vitamin/supplement. Not all brands are the same! Not all bodies are the same.

During the Day

PUSH FEAR OUT! Whenever it comes up within you or if it is reflected to you in someone else (a mirror back to you!), push it out. Find something that excites you and immerse yourself in it. Breathe! Visualize yourself in perfect health. Find joy in life. Move out of fear and into love. Focus on what you want, not what you don't want. The more you focus on something, the more you create it. Create love, not fear.

Find something you can do throughout the course of the day that carries compassionate action. **Compassionate action** is when you see someone or a situation and stop for a moment to send positive thoughts. You can send healing energy. It will go wherever you want it to go. Do this in a group for more powerful results. What you give out will come back to you.

Follow your passion, whatever it is that excites you, no matter how great or how small it may be at the time.

Smile and laugh often (no pretending!). Laughter is the best medicine.

Find joy in life. If you don't have anything that brings you joy, create it. You are a creator! The best way to manifest positive results is through joy. Find joy, no matter how brief, even in the midst of depression. Joy will help to raise your vibration.

Spend time saying decrees or positive affirmations. A decree always begins with "I Am." They are very powerful. Always make sure the words that follow are positive to create a happy life filled with love.

Break negative behavior patterns. Change your routine. Take yourself off "autopilot." Leave the house through a different door. Take a different route on your way to work. It's time to break old behavior patterns and habits.

Monitor your thoughts, words, and actions. What are you creating (drawing to you) as a result of your words and actions? Do your best to remain positive in everything you think, say, and do. The best way to move through life's challenges is by staying positive.

Recite your own personal I Am decrees to promote healing. For example:
- I Am in Perfect Health and Well-Being.
- I Am Healing NOW. I Am Releasing all-dis-ese from my body NOW.
- I Am Grateful for ...

When adversity comes knocking at your door, take a step back. Breathe. Be the observer. What is really going on? When you feel it in your gut, if you get upset, it's your "stuff." Look at the whole picture, not just what you want to see. Take time to go within. You are in this situation for a reason. What do you need to learn from it? What are your fears? What are you trying to control? What are you getting out of the situation? Do you have an attachment to the outcome? Are you placing expectations on someone who cannot meet them? Change your perspective. Diffuse the situation and move forward.

If something comes up to challenge your peace, walk away and take a few deep cleansing breaths. Respond from love. Do not react (going into fear).

Look for the best in everyone you meet, especially in those you dislike. Never gossip or spread rumors. Gossip does more damage than it does good, and it is karmic. What goes around comes around. How will you feel when you are on the receiving end? You may be on the receiving end now. Walk away. Let it go. Do not let anything take away your peace. It is not worth it.

Be courteous and polite. Take time to smile, especially to someone who needs it most.

Be in service whenever possible. Do everything from the heart, expecting nothing in return (even so much as a "thank you"). Being in service does not mean being a doormat or enabler. Boundaries with consequences are important to maintaining balance in the relationship.

Rest a few minutes several times throughout the day to clear your mind.

Breathe! Take a couple of nice, deep cleansing breaths to let go of stress. Detach from any negative emotions that may arise.

Go for a walk daily to get some fresh air and to help eliminate toxins from the body.

Play games or read high vibrational material to keep your mind sharp.

Maintain a state of peace and calm the best that you can. When life throws a curve ball, spend three to five minutes giving gratitude or saying I Am decrees to shift you in a more positive way.

Before Retiring at Night

Use Castor Oil Packs where tumors are present to help dissolve them. (See "Castor Oil Packs" under "Tools to Enhance Good Health and Well-Being" for more information.)

Review your day. What was the best part of your day? What could you have done better? What did you accomplish? What still needs to be done? Write your thoughts down for a better night's sleep.

Release stress to ensure a restful night's sleep. Left unchecked, it can disrupt various physiological processes.

Thank God each and every night for all of the things you have had, have, and will have. Thank God for the healing taking place to bring you back to a better version of you. Give gratitude for the many blessings received that day. Give gratitude for lessons learned.

Breathe. Take a few slow, deep breaths to release stress to sleep better. Ask your guides to help find the answers you are looking for while you sleep.

Weekly

Test your pH weekly with the pH litmus strips. Do this in the morning before you eat. Drink water or rinse your mouth to clear old saliva from the night before, then use a test strip about 15 minutes after.

Juice three times a week. Make a smoothie containing fruits and vegetables high in anti-cancer properties and packed with antioxidants and vitamin C to help protect cells from cell damage.

Exercise regularly at least three to four times a week for thirty to sixty minutes. This can be dancing, gardening, or swimming. Go for a brisk walk to get some fresh air. If you are over forty, use a treadmill or elliptical to keep your cardiovascular system healthy. A regular exercise routine can help improve metabolic function and remove acid waste products from the body.

Periodically

Do a raw vegetable and water cleanse for three days. Everyone should this twice a year to cleanse the digestive system.

Smudge your house with sage to release all negative, fear-based energy. Clear your home with sound (play music or ring a bell) to keep your house clear, especially after a trauma. Your home should be your safe haven for peace and healing.

Write Release Letters whenever you get upset or triggered. Where did the emotion come from? Why is it there? What do you need to learn from it? When you feel an emotion in your gut, it's your "stuff." Pay attention! There is something you need to look at. Your gut is your warning sign. When you feel it in your heart, it is love. Keep releasing to raise your vibration! It will help raise your vibration. (See "Tools to Enhance Good Health and Well-Being)

Release Emotional Trauma whenever necessary and as often as possible. You'll be surprised at what comes up! Maintain a sense of peace and calm. (See "Tools to Enhance Good Health and Well-Being)

Pamper yourself! Schedule an **Ionic Foot Detox** to release toxins from the body. If taking chemotherapy, have an Ionic Foot Detox done the day before your chemo session to release toxins from the body. If the toxins are not released, gravity will pull them to the feet, creating neuropathy in the feet. When you have finished chemotherapy, have an Ionic Foot Detox at least once a week for the next three to five weeks to flush out chemo from the body.

Lay on the **Quantum Resonance Crystal Bed** to regenerate all of the cells in the body. An effective protocol consists of laying on the bed for five weeks, twice a week, one hour each time. Clients typically notice a big change in their bodies by the end of the third week. Once the protocol is finished, lay on the bed once or twice a month for maintenance purposes.

Experience an energy or sound healing session periodically (biweekly or monthly, no less) to keep your energy in balance. Recommended services include: Reiki, Quantum Healing, QXCI/SCIO biofeedback consciousness, massage, reflexology, crystal surgery, past-life regression, etc.

Alkalize Your Body

Start your day with a tall glass of water with a hint of lemon to boost your metabolism and provide energy for proper hydration and oxygenation and mental clarity. Add a teaspoon of honey for even healthier results.

Alkalize your body by adding one teaspoon of natural baking soda to a cup of warm water. Drink it first thing in the morning to alkalize your body and promote increased energy and overall well-being.

Eat a handful of almonds. They are rich in natural alkaline minerals, such as calcium and magnesium, and can help balance blood sugar and the blood's pH level.

Use turmeric whenever possible. Turmeric is a spice grown in many Asian countries. Curcumin, a substance in turmeric, has been proven to kill cancer cells in certain kinds of cancer. Turmeric may have side effects if taken in large amounts. Research on curcumin as a cancer treatment is ongoing.[89]

Eat alkaline-forming foods. Maintain an 80 percent alkaline/20 percent acid diet. Eat plenty of fresh fruits and nuts, peas and beans, sweet potatoes and yams, green vegetables (like Brussel sprouts), and fresh, leafy types of vegetables. Green leafy vegetables are high in vitamins, minerals, and antioxidants. Reduce your intake of acidic foods to help manage pH levels and preserve bone density, prevent kidney stones, and eliminate symptoms of acid reflux.

Eliminate processed foods and processed sugar from your diet. These include sodas, artificial sweeteners, candy, cakes, cookies, artificial sweeteners, etc., especially processed sugars that are high fructose corn syrup, artificial sugar, corn syrup solids, fructose, sucrose, and dextrose. They are very acidic. Even ketchup, yogurt, and pasta sauce are full of sugar and can contribute to an imbalanced pH in the blood.

Reduce caffeine found in coffee and other "pick me up" drinks. They are acidic.

Limit tobacco and alcohol intake. Alcohol changes your pH by altering the liver and kidneys' ability to function properly. One to two glasses a day will not hurt, especially if it is a glass of red wine. Red wine contains powerful antioxidants which can boost heart, gut, and brain health. Everything should be taken in moderation to maintain proper balance in life.[90]

---

[89] https://www.cancerresearchuk.org/about-cancer/treatment/complementary-alternative-therapies/individual-therapies/turmeric
[90] https://www.medicalnewstoday.com/articles/265635

Drink Fiji, spring, mineral, alkaline, Kangen®, or John Ellis water. Drink enough water to help flush toxins out of the body but not so much as to flush nutrients out of the body. Try not to drink purified water.

Drink herbal teas, such as Essiac, dandelion, ginger, moringa, and soursop, to help cleanse and detox the body, release inflammation, and support the immune system.

When possible, **put 15 drops of the ISO water and 15 drops of the John Ellis water** in 6 oz. of water, then drink it. Repeat this procedure three times a day (morning, noon, and evening) the first week, then back off to two times a day (morning and evening) after the first week.

Diffuse Frankincense essential oil (premium grade, 4-5 drops) while you sleep at night. Place a drop of Frankincense oil on the appropriate reflexology points on the feet and hands several times a day. Frankincense oil is a powerful essential oil that can assist in releasing cancer.

Use Young Living's Release essential oil on the appropriate reflexology points of the feet and hands. Set the intention to release all dis-ease from the body.

Use Canadian Forest Tree Essences—Letting Go, Deep Inner Cleansing, Guilt and Forgiveness, and Healing the Heart—daily, 2-3 times a day, to release the emotions of anger and resentment, jealousy and envy, grieving and depression. Vibrational Tree Essences can enhance emotional and spiritual well-being. Take no more than three tree essences at a time.

Body test to know what is best for your fourfold body. Your body knows what it needs to maintain good health and well-being.

And remember, tools are no good if you don't use them!

Tools to Enhance Good Health and Well-Being

How ironic that today people are fed information by the food industry which pays no attention to health and are treated by the health industry which pays no attention to food.

The following is information on healing remedies, teas, essences, and more to assist in releasing an overage of cancer in the fourfold body. Be sure to give gratitude daily for the healing taking place. And remember, tools are no good if you don't use them!

Sound and Vibrational Healing

"Science is not only compatible with spirituality; it is a profound source of spirituality. The notion that science and spirituality are somehow mutually exclusive does a disservice to both." ~ Carl Sagan (1934-1996), American Astronomer and author of the book, *The Demon-Haunted World: Science as a Candle in the Dark* [91]

Everything in our universe is made of sound and vibration. The body is a network of vibrational fields and energy currents. The colors of the rainbow correspond to a specific musical note in the same way each chakra of the body corresponds with a particular tone or color.

The vibration of sound causes our cells to move in different directions at a different speed. It penetrates our cells and rebalances them through oscillation and resonance, bringing harmony to the body. Even those who cannot hear can benefit from sound healing.

Sound can transform every part of our being, physically, emotionally, and spiritually. The healing power of sound can have a powerful effect on the way we feel. Dr. Gaynor's research shows that the sound vibration of the bowls affects the dysrhythmic motion found in cancer cells, causing a harmonious transformation.

---

[91] https://www.goodreads.com/quotes/44909-science-is-not-only-compatible-with-spirituality-it-is-a

Listening to crystal bowls helps to balance the chakra system and release blockages in all 32 layers of the human aura, reenergizing the auric field so that healing can be achieved on all levels. Each person is unique and different. Depending on what is going on in their life, they may find themselves being drawn to different tones of the bowls.

When energy practitioners use sound in their sessions, clients immediately go into a state of full receptivity and relaxation. This allows the practitioner to go deeper and more easily reach underlying issues.

Science is beginning to take note as to what those in the alternative medicine field have known for a long time—that certain rhythms and sounds can influence the way we feel. Sound healing not only helps to reduce anxiety, stress, and depression, it can help to heal the whole—mind, body, and spirit.

According to the National Center for Biotechnology Information, heart disease, diabetes, addiction, and mental health issues have all been linked to stress and tension. Meditation, including sound vibration meditations, has shown promise in inducing the relaxation response necessary to help alleviate anxiety and improve well-being. The relaxation response is the body's physiological response in relaxation, including lowered blood pressure to counter the fight-or-flight response and activation of the parasympathetic nervous system. This study examined the effects of sound meditation on mood, anxiety, pain, and spiritual well-being. Feeling of spiritual well-being significantly increased across all participants. [92]

Dr. Mitchell Gaynor, a medical oncologist, was a pioneer of Integrative Oncology. He founded Gaynor Integrative Oncology in Manhattan. Dr. Gaynor used state-of-the-art cancer treatment, along with additional complementary therapies including sound, such as Tibetan singing bowls, crystal singing bowls, changing, meditation, nutrition and supplements.

According to Dr. Gaynor, "If we accept that sound is vibration and we know that vibration touches every part of our physical being, then

---

[92] https://www.ncbi.nlm.nih.gov/pmc/articles/PMC5871151/

we understand that sound is heard not only through our ears but through every cell in our bodies."

Dr. Gaynor viewed sound "as part of a broader trend toward the humanization of medicine in which the whole person, not just the part that's broken, is addressed." He believed "sound can play a role in virtually any medical disorder, since it redresses imbalances on every level of physiologic functioning."

He was the author of several books including The Healing Power of Sound (1999), Dr. Gaynor's Cancer Prevention Program (1999), Healing Essence (2000), Nurture Nature, Nurture Health (2005) and The Gene Therapy Plan (2015).[93]

More and more, sound healing is being recognized for its many benefits. It is on its way to becoming mainstream, like yoga and meditation. The rhythms, tones, and vibrations of music can slow down breathing, brain waves, and heart rates.

The next time you need a little balancing in your life, hum a tune or go for a walk in the park—experience Nature's own healing harmonies! There's nothing better to bring about a deep feeling of peace and sense of well-being.

Herbal Remedies

Herbs have played an important role in humanity's history. They have been used for cooking and medicinal purposes. Herbs found their way into linen closets because of their pleasant fragrances, and they were used to dye homespun fabrics and leather. Herb gardens were an essential part of pioneer homes.

As more and more people become aware of the dangers of synthetic drugs and medications, herbal remedies are on the rise. Home remedies using herbs are considerably cheaper than prescription medicines and rarely have any side effects. Herbs can be easily grown outside in a garden or inside in a flowerpot.

Popular herbs to keep on hand are mint, chamomile, thyme, and lemon balm.

---

[93] https://www.strang.org/mitchell-l-gaynor-md

155

Mint, often used as a breath freshener, has been reported to help maintain a healthy digestive system and calm stomach aches. Ginger can help calm the stomach, ease the build-up of gases, and increase circulation.

Chamomile is perfect for relaxation and a good sleep. It can ease colic and anxiety issues. Thyme can help relieve stomach cramps due to gas build-up, and lemon balm has been used in the treatment of colds and the flu. Lemon balm can help to heal scrapes, minor cuts, and insect bites. It can also help with anxiety and insomnia.

Tiger balm, nutmeg oil, feverfew, passion flower, lemon balm, and peppermint oil work to help relieve headaches. Ginkgo biloba works to help improve circulation and reduce inflammation.

While most herbal remedies enhance the body's natural ability to heal through rebalancing and cleansing, there are some that can be dangerous when taken with synthetic medicine. Be sure to consult a knowledgeable practitioner before taking remedial herbs.

Herbal Teas

Herbal teas have been around for hundreds of years in China, Asia, and Japan and are a natural healing drink that can be served hot or cold. There are sipping teas, and there are healing teas. Most teas have less caffeine than coffee. People are beginning to drink more teas like green tea, oolong tea, white tea, and black tea than coffee or soft drinks because of their medicinal purposes and pleasant flavor.

Traditional teas (such as green, black, white, and oolong teas) are made from the dried young leaves and leaf buds of the tea bush (Camelilia sinensis). Herbal teas are not made from the tea bush. They are made from an infusion of flowers, spices, herbs, leaves, seeds, bark, fruits, berries, spices, and plant roots.

Essiac Tea®

Essiac Tea®, given its name by Rene Caisse ("Caisse" spelt backwards), consists of four main herbs that grow in the wilderness of Ontario, Canada. The original formula is believed to have its roots from the native Canadian Ojibway Indians.

The four main herbs that make up Essiac are Burdock Root, Slippery Elm Inner Bark, Sheep Sorrel and Indian Rhubarb Root.

Burdock root: This root contains compounds shown to promote blood circulation, improve skin texture and stabilize blood sugar.

Slippery elm: Revered for its medicinal properties, slippery elm is rich in disease-fighting antioxidants and may aid in treating inflammatory bowel disease.

Sheep sorrel: Also known by its scientific name, *Rumex acetosella,* sheep sorrel has been shown to have potent antiviral properties in test-tube studies.

Indian rhubarb: One recent animal study found that Indian rhubarb is high in antioxidants and may inhibit the growth of liver cancer cells in rats.

Essiac Tea® has had a long history of assisting patients to release cancer and live life. No extensive clinical studies have been performed as yet which would provide conclusive evidence that Rene Caisse's herbal formula will alleviate, cure or prevent any disease or condition.

Nurse Rene Caisse spent most of her career defending herself against the medical and government establishments. She believed she was never imprisoned only because of the overwhelming popular support of her work and the fact that she had such well-documented stories. At one point she even took on Parliament itself. Rene Caisse continues to be loved and remembered for her contribution to naturopathic medicine.

Essiac Tea® is usually sold in powder form, but capsule and tea bag varieties are also available. For more information on Essiac Tea®, visit http://us.essiactea.org.

Dandelion Tea

This tea can be brewed using whole dandelion plants or just the leaves, roots, or stems. People can brew dandelion tea at home or find it in health-food stores.

Dandelion tea contains nutrients, such as vitamin A, that can be beneficial to a person's health. Dandelion tea offers an alternative for people who want to stop drinking caffeinated beverages, such as coffee and black tea, or limit their daily consumption.

Research suggests that all parts of the dandelion plant contain many natural anti-inflammatory and antioxidant compounds. According to the National Institutes of Health (NIH), people have used dandelion in traditional medicine for years, believing that it can treat health problems relating to the liver, gallbladder, and bile duct. Its diuretic effect means the tea encourages both urination and reduced water retention in the body. Dandelion tea can also help to cleanse the liver and release inflammation.

Ginger Tea

Ginger is known as the universal medicine, and ginger tea is known for its many health benefits. Tea made from ginger has high levels of vitamin C and amino acids, as well as various trace elements such as calcium, zinc, sodium, phosphorus, and many others.

Drinking ginger tea can:
- Help the body absorb nutrients
- Help alleviate the stomach pain
- Help with irritable bowel syndrome
- Help with weight loss
- Help release cancer
- Help manage glucose levels
- Improve circulation
- Improve the food digestion
- Increases the production of gastric juice
- Protect against Alzheimer's Disease
- Open inflamed airways
- Reduce arthritic inflammation
- Relieve menstrual discomfort
- Relieve stress
- Stimulate appetite

Drinking ginger tea—2 to 3 cups daily, especially before meals—can be useful to help stimulate slow digestion and sharpen dull taste buds.

Soursop Tea

Soursop tea, also called Graviola tea, is an herbal tea made from the leaves of the soursop fruit tree native to tropical areas in North and

South America. The fruit and leaves contain antioxidants such as flavonoids, phytosterols, and tannins. Studies suggest that soursop has both chemopreventive and therapeutic potential.

In addition to its anticancer properties, soursop tea has been used to treat infections, coughs, weight loss, herpes, inflammation of the nose and throat, and parasitic infections such as lice. Soursop tea or soursop fruit have also been used to induce vomiting or to increase relaxation.[94]

Memorial Sloan Kettering Cancer Center advises not to consume soursop or soursop leaves if you take blood pressure or diabetes medication, or if you will be having nuclear imaging performed. They also warn repeated use may cause liver and kidney toxicity and that side effects of soursop may include movement disorders and myeloneuropathy (a condition with symptoms similar to Parkinson's disease).[95]

Moringa Tea

Moringa tea gets its nutrients from the dried moringa leaves, which may be abundant in potassium, calcium, phosphorus, iron, and vitamins A, C, and D. The tea may also have high levels of essential amino acids, antioxidants such as beta-carotene, polyphenols, and flavonoids such as kaempferol and quercetin. Moringa tea does not contain caffeine.

Health benefits may include:
- Aid in weight loss
- Energy booster
- Anti-inflammatory properties
- High in antioxidants
- Beneficial for skin care
- Boost the immune system
- Manage diabetes
- Aid in digestion
- Improve healing rate
- Boost cognition

---

[94] https://www.verywellfit.com/soursop-tea-benefits-and-side-effects-4163737#citation-2
[95] Graviola. Memorial Sloan Kettering Cancer Center. 2019

- Balance hormones
- Relieve menstrual cramps
- Contain antimicrobial and antibacterial properties
- Protect against arsenic toxicity
- Boost sex drive
- Promote hair growth
- Increase milk production in nursing mothers

There are no commonly seen side effects or toxic components of moringa tea, provided you drink it in moderate amounts. If there are side effects, they may include:

- Heartburn
- Nausea
- Diarrhea
- Risk of miscarriage[96]

Healing teas have medicinal properties that have been reported to cleanse and detoxify, alleviate pain, reduce fever, induce sweating, boost the immune system, fight infection, calm the stomach, fight cancer, ease spasms, support the heart and liver, cause vomiting, induce coughing to bring up phlegm, calm the nerves, help with insomnia, and much more. They work over a period of time.

Healing teas have been used in baths, as poultices, and as tinctures. They can be a natural way to bring the body's internal systems back into balance.

Essential Oils

A living plant can assist in living life. Essential oils were one of the first medicines used by man. Egyptian and Chinese manuscripts show they have been used for thousands of years. They are mentioned in the Bible many times. The three Wise Men gave frankincense and myrrh to baby Jesus.

Essential oils are created from the natural aromatic volatile liquids in plants (i.e., shrubs, flowers, trees, roots, bushes, and seeds). These

---

[96] https://www.organicfacts.net/health-benefits/herbs-and-spices/moringa-tea.html

liquids contain the life force of the plant. Pure, premium-grade essential oils are best because they are distilled from plants. The purity of the oil will determine how they will work with your body.

Aromatherapy

Pure, organic essential oils are used in aromatherapy to assist in treating dis-ease. Fragrances stimulate nerves in the nose, sending impulses to the brain which control memory and emotion. This process stimulates and calms the body. Essential oils assist the body to awaken and strengthen an individual's natural energies.

Using Essential Oils

Always use pure, organic essential oils. Test an essential oil on the skin before using an essential oil. Each person's body is different. Apply one drop of oil on the skin and wait 3-5 minutes for the body to respond. Use pure vegetable oil to dilute the oil on the skin if discomfort or skin irritation is caused.

Methods for Using Essential Oils

- *Topical*—applied directly to the skin
- *Diffuse*—Diffused oils increase oxygen availability. Many essential oils are effective in eliminating and destroying airborne germs and bacteria.
- *Bath or shower*—It is best to use essential oils diluted in Dead Sea salts when bathing. An undiluted essential can sometimes cause discomfort on sensitive skin because the oils float on top of the water.
- *Compress*—Rub 1-3 drops of essential oil on the afflicted area. Cover the area with a hot, damp towel. Cover the moist towel with a dry towel for 10-30 minutes, depending on the need. If patient has neurological conditions, use cool water. For sensitive skin, place 5-15 drops of essential oil into a bowl. Stir the water vigorously and let stand for one minute. Place a dry wash cloth on top of the water to soak up the oils that have floated to the surface. Wring out the water and apply cloth to afflicted area. To seal in warmth, cover with a thick towel for 15-30 minutes.

- *Inhale*—Place 2-3 drops of essential oil in one hand. Rub both hands together. Breathe in (deeply) through the nose and breathe out through the mouth. Do this 3-4 times.
- *Layering*— applying multiple oils, one at a time, ending with Peppermint to drive the others in faster

Essential Oils to Help Release Cancer

Essential oils that can help to release cancer, inflammation, infection, and pain from the body include:
- to release cancer: frankincense, sandalwood, lavender, arborvitae, Young Living's Release essential oil
- to release infection: cinnamon, clary sage, bergamot, myrrh (with oregano), Douglas Fir.
- to release inflammation: frankincense, melaleuca, eucalyptus, and oregano.
- to oxygenate the blood: sandalwood, frankincense
- to release pain: lavender, eucalyptus, doTerra's Deep Blue rub
- to release tumors: frankincense[97]

Keep essential oils out of reach of children and away from eyes and ears. Do not touch your eyes with your hands after touching essential oils.

Pregnant women and epileptics should always check with an open-minded healthcare professional when starting any type of health program. Many healthcare providers do not approve of natural ways to heal. (See Appendix, Essential Oils for Healing)

Castor Oil Packs

Castor oil is a thick, page yellow oil extracted from the seeds of the castor oil plant, also known as *Ricinus communis*. Castor oil packs consist of a piece of fabric soaked in castor oil and then applied to certain areas of the body. Edgar Cayce recommended castor oil packs to eradicate tumors near the breast surface.[98]

---

[97] *Modern Essentials*, © 2016 AromaTools™, 8th edution, 2nd printing, February 2017. All rights reserved.
[98] https://www.ncbi.nlm.nih.gov/pmc/articles/PMC4327996/

Castor oil packs promote detoxification, lower inflammation, and support female reproductive health. Castor oil can improve the hair and skin due to its moisturizing, antimicrobial properties. It is particularly beneficial for skin conditions such as eczema, psoriasis, and dermatitis.

Due to its anti-inflammatory qualities, castor oil can help reduce joint pain and enhance joint mobility when applied topically.[99]

Earth-based Healing

Everything we need to heal can be found in Nature. Earth-based healing is natural and free or relatively inexpensive. Following are a few methods that can assist in healing:

- Use topsoil (not potting soil) to release inflammation in the body. Place feet in a pan of topsoil so they are completely covered. Add one cup of water to make a poultice. Put the poultice around the ankles. Keep feet in the dirt until tingling is felt in the legs or a deep sigh is experienced. If inflammation is experienced in the legs, sprinkle one teaspoon of dried thyme (representing all time, space, and dimensions) and one teaspoon of dried fennel (the funnel) to the dirt. Do this once a day as long as needed.
- When dis-ease is on or near the arm, take some topsoil (not potting soil) and mix it with a little bit of water to make a poultice. Put the wet dirt on a sheet of plastic wrap, then wrap the mud around the arm and hold it there for about ten minutes or until a tingling in the arm or a deep sigh is experienced. A little bit of cinnamon can also be sprinkled (don't mix it in the dirt) on the dirt so that the cinnamon is between the dirt and the arm before it is packed around the arm. Do this at least twice a day, if possible. Cinnamon is good for releasing inflammation.
- Drink a glass of water with a teaspoon of cinnamon and a teaspoon of local honey to help release inflammation in the body.

---

[99] https://www.drberg.com/blog/castor-oil-packs

- One way to help release a fibroid tumor is to get a lemon. Cut it in half and in half again, then into slices. Every day while in the shower, take two of the lemon slices and rub them over the area where the tumor is located and say, "I Am releasing everything that I am fearful of. I release any memories I don't want to look at." Go up and down, back and forth, and then in a circle—counterclockwise—and then clockwise using the two lemon slices, going over the area where the fibroid tumors are.
- Squeeze lemon slices over the afflicted area and let the juice run over the skin. Repeat again saying, "I Am releasing all fear that is causing these tumors." Use a new lemon every day. Do this for five days in the shower. Also thump three times on top of the fibroid tumor to help break it up.
- Many people believe when cancer goes to the lymph nodes, they will die. This does not have to happen. Be careful! If you believe it will happen, you can create it.
- Take a grapefruit and peel it. Separate the sections. Take the sections apart so the little pockets in each section can be pinched. Pinch each pocket to release the juice and what is being held emotionally in the lymph nodes. Pressure will be felt when this is done. When you don't feel pressure when pinching sections, you are done. This can also be done with an orange, but a grapefruit works better.
- Drink lemon juice in water to cleanse the body.

Earthing

Earthing, also known as grounding, is part of Nature's design. According to Dr. Gaétan Chevalier, it refers to "the discovery that contact with the Earth's electric energy generates significant physiological changes in the body, including reduction of inflammation and pain, a shift in the autonomic nervous system from sympathetic (stress and vigilance) to parasympathetic (more relaxed and calm), a thinning of the blood, better sleep, and more energy."

Dr. Chevalier has said, "Animals are naturally in contact with the surface of the earth. Plants, obviously so. Humans, hardly at all anymore. Unlike our ancestors, we do not walk barefoot very much.

We don't sleep on the ground. Today, we wear synthetic soled shoes that insulate us from the earth's electric energy. We no longer live and work on the ground. Our homes and workplaces are elevated off the ground, and often very high off the ground. Simply stated, we are disconnected. And, based on our research, this disconnect may actually be a totally overlooked contributor to the epidemic of inflammation at the basis of so many common diseases and even the aging process itself."

Additional benefits of earthing may include: reduces blood viscosity (a major factor in cardiovascular disease), improves inflammation and blood flow, and reduces muscle damage after moderate exercise.

Grounding can be as simple as being barefoot outside on conductive surfaces such as grass, sand, soil, and concrete, or indoors while sitting or sleeping in contact with conductive mats, bands, and patches.

More information can be found in the book, *Earthing*. For information on the full studies, visit www.earthinginstitute.net. Indoor grounding products can be purchased at www.earthing.com.[100]

Flower Remedies

The system of plant and flower-based essences was developed in the 1930s by Dr. Edward Bach, a physician and homeopath who was convinced that emotional well-being was key to overall health.

Dr. Bach devoted his life to exploring the use of flowers and plants to create a simple, natural and gentle approach to emotional balance. He eventually went on to establish The Bach Centre in Oxfordshire, England, where he developed the essences as we know them today.

As demand for the essences grew, The Bach Centre partnered with Nelsons Pharmacy to help make and bottle the essences, and Nelsons has been responsible for the signature brand essences ever since. Nelsons is the owner of the Bach® Original Flower Remedy brand, and is the only maker authorized by The Bach Center.

---

[100] https://www.chi.is/healing-with-the-earth/

The most famous of all Bach remedies is Rescue Remedy, a blend of five different Bach flower remedies. Rescue Remedy was created by Dr. Bach to deal with emergencies, grief, trauma, crisis, or stressful situations. It can be used to help us get through any stressful situations, from last-minute exams or interview nerves to the aftermath of an accident or bad news. Rescue Remedy can help us relax, be focused, and get the needed calmness to cope with stress.[101]

MAP: The Co-Creative White Brotherhood Medical Assistance Program is an excellent book detailing a comprehensive medical program for humans using flower remedies. It addresses our general health; any specific illness, disease or condition; injuries (serious or small); our mental health; our emotional health; and our overall well-being. As a program, it couldn't be more simple. With MAP you have high quality medical assistance any time day or night. This book is available for purchase on Amazon.

For more information or to purchase Bach Flower Remedies, visit www.bachremedies.com.

Tree Essences

Vibrational Tree Essences are subtle liquid extracts usually taken orally to nurture emotional and spiritual well-being. They act by nourishing the energy field of a person or animal via their positive resonance, and in doing so, they help us maintain inner balance.

Canadian Forest tree essences are liquid preparations—usually taken orally (or added to water, a bath, a mist, oil or other carrier) used to address unresolved emotional issues that underly mind-body health, augment our personal resonance and sense of well-being, and nourish our inner development.

They are effective tools to fill a gap in the healing spectrum. They are powerful, natural frequency in a bottle, with no side effect, for helping resolve and overcome emotional issues, bring out the natural strength within, and accelerate the process of healing along with any other modalities available.

---

[101] https://www.bachremedies.com/en-ca/about/our-story/

Vibrational tree essences are not traditional herbal remedies used for physical healing. Nor are vibrational tree essences the same as essential oils, which contain the concentrated chemical fragrance from a plant valued for both its physical and emotional effect.

Instead, vibrational tree essences, like flower and gem essences, are designed to act solely through their frequency and resonance supporting us emotionally and energetically. Vibrational tree essences are not a treatment for any specific disease or disorder.

Tree essences are part of the growing field of energy medicine, which also includes homeopathy, music and sound therapy, light and color therapy, and related modalities.

Tree essences are prepared following a modified protocol of that developed originally by the English physician Edward Bach in the 1930's, best known for his "Rescue Remedy."

The tree essences, like homeopathic preparations, contain infinitesimal amounts of substances and are safe to use. They are effective in helping to reframe the way we perceive life, world events and circumstances, to break emotional states or unconscious patterns that hold us in their grip, and to raise our vibration for greater well-being.

The tree essences support body-mind through their resonance as trees are a vibrational presence just like human beings and all living beings. The tree essences awaken positive vibrations, nourishing all areas of resonance within us.

Taking a vibrational tree essence is like giving water to our inner garden. Vibrational tree essences enliven our awareness and attention, facilitating a process of reflection and attunement, and an opening and deepening of understanding.

The result of taking vibrational tree essences is to attune to the natural intelligence and rhythms of nature. We feel stronger and more able to take on challenges.

Canadian Forest tree essences support us in resolving a range of emotional issues. Using vibrational tree essences, insight is brought to bear on unwanted patterns, allowing them to be cleared from our psyche. We feel ourselves letting go, opening, relaxing, being freer, more flowing, and able to access our inner healing resources.

Use "Letting Go," "Deep Inner Cleansing," and/or "Guilt and Forgiveness" Canadian Forest Tree Essences daily, 2-3 times a day, to release emotions of anger, resentment, and grieving. Take no more than three tree essences at a time.[102]

For more information or to purchase Canadian Forest Tree Essences, visit www.essences.ca.

Crystals and Minerals

Crystals are amazing! They can focus, absorb, and transmit subtle electromagnetic energy. They can also amplify energy. The energy from quartz crystals can operate computers, radios, watches, and many other digital and electronic devices.

Crystals vibrate at fixed, stable, and unchangeable frequencies. Humans are the opposite. Our energy fluctuates, depending on our emotional state at the time. When we feel loving and positive, our vibration rises. When we feel depressed, angry, or any other negative emotion, our vibration lowers.

Crystals are also conductors of energy and can assist in the healing process. By placing crystals near or on the body, the vibration of the crystal interacts with and changes our vibration, helping to bring us back into balance. When all the spirit bodies are in balance, healing flows into the physical body.

Most minerals are crystalline in structure. Some grow large, depending on the space, and some remain small. Some of the more common crystals are mined, such as emeralds, rubies, sapphires, and diamonds. Some crystals are created from living organisms, such as pearls or amber. Crystals can be as hard as a diamond or as fragile as selenite.

Minerals cannot be produced by the body, and yet all bodily processes depend on the action and interaction of minerals. One mineral shortage can create an imbalance in the physical body. Minerals are more important than vitamins because vitamins can be synthesized by living matter. Minerals cannot.

---

[102] https://essences.ca/

When a crystal is placed on the physical body, minerals from the crystal can be absorbed by the body to be used as needed. Sodium helps regulate water in the body's blood and tissue. Iron helps the blood and muscles carry oxygen to the body, and zinc helps wounds to heal.

Copper, iron, and zinc are metals that can also aid the physical body. For instance, copper helps the nerves to function and red blood cells to form. It helps to maintain energy levels and helps build strong bones and energizes the immune system.

Copper has been used for centuries to treat arthritis and rheumatic conditions. Wearing copper can help improve blood circulation, increase energy, reduce inflammation, stabilize metabolism, expel toxins from the body, improve oxygen use, prevent thyroid problems, promote healthy skin and hair, and it can also work to prevent heart problems by regulating blood pressure and heart rate. Copper also absorbs iron from the gut, and it is used to make many important compounds in the body.

Magnets have been known to relieve arthritis pain, stress headaches and migraines, improve blood circulation, stimulate metabolism, alter nerve impulses, reverse degenerative diseases, increase the flow of oxygen to cells, decrease fatty deposits on artery walls, and realign thought patterns to improve emotional well-being.

Magnets also help to heal cuts, infections, and broken bones, and have been known to help cure cancer by decreasing acidity in the body. Cancer cells cannot survive in a highly alkaline body. Magnets also reverse the effects of toxic chemicals, addictive drugs, and other harmful substances found in the body.

Many energy practitioners use crystals and metals during an energy session. The practitioner intuits which crystals would best serve to assist in a client's healing process, then places them on the body during a session. Some practitioners even use crystals as tools to remove negative energy and heal the spirit body.

More and more, crystals and metals are being recognized for the role they play in healing and in bringing about peace.

Crystals that can help to release anger include:
- *Faden Quartz* are Tabular (Tabby) Quartz Crystals that have a milky white thread-like line of growth running edge to

edge through the crystal. A Faden Quartz crystal enhances self-healing and provides a direction for personal growth, the integration of fragmented soul parts, and balances emotional stability. The thread within can pull out past emotions that no longer have a purpose. Place the stone with the thread along the finger or pointing out from the afflicted area. Be sure to place a Platinum Flame on the other end of the stone so the emotions being released can be transmuted into love. Hold stone in place for 3-5 minutes until a deep breath is experienced. This is the release you are looking for. Hold the faden in place or move to another finger or area for as long as needed.

- *Carnelian* can help express your opinions effectively while encouraging others to work as a team. Carnelian helps to accept change, healing relationships with others and with the self.
- *Amethyst* can help to reduce inflamed emotions and transmute anger into peace and tranquility. This powerful yet protective stone facilitates decision-making and brings in common sense and spiritual insight.
- *Rose Quartz* can help you to love yourself by eliminating aggression, releasing jealousy and resentfulness. Rose Quartz encourages acceptance and unconditional love.
- *Peridot* can help to release blame, shame, and guilt. Peridot is a powerful cleanser, releasing toxins on all levels.
- *Muscovite* can help to release our own insecurities that can be projected towards others as judgement and condemnation. Muscovite encourages acceptance and unconditional love.
- *Smoky Quartz* is excellent for treating radiation-related illness or chemotherapy. It can provide pain relief. Point away from the body to draw off negative energies; towards to body to energize.

To help release cancer, you may want to wear/carry a medicine bag consisting of one or more crystals that assist in releasing an overage of cancer. (See Appendix, Crystals That Assist in Releasing Cancer.)

Release Letters

An overage of cancer in the physical body represents an excess of anger and resentment held deep within us. The more one gives into anger and resentment, the more they fuel the dis-ease. Whenever you feel anger and resentment, write a release letter to clear these emotions. Like a weed, if you don't get to the root, it will come back thicker and stronger.

You cannot change what happened, but you can change how you feel about what happened. Releasing emotions and situations heals all wounds. True release comes from the heart. It frees the soul to move on. Words are easily spoken, but not always meant.

Apologize for whatever you may have contributed to the situation, intentionally or unintentionally, and release whoever may have hurt you. And don't forget to apologize to yourself for your lack of understanding. If you are the victim, you were probably the perpetrator at some point in time. You may be getting back something you once gave out (karma).

Many people pray to God for forgiveness because it is much easier to ask God than to face the person we hurt. Apologize to the person(s) hurt. You do not need God's forgiveness for, in Truth, you have never done anything wrong—only experienced! God understands both parties are learning lessons through your experiences. It is important to apologize to the person you hurt.

Accept responsibility for your mistake and work to heal the situation. If the person you need to apologize to has crossed over, write a release letter to him or her anyway. It will benefit both of you.

Releasing is a requirement if true and lasting change is desired. (See Appendix, Release Letters)

Self-Healing Techniques

Following are a few self-healing techniques you can do on yourself or for someone else:

Release Stress

A few ways to release stress, especially in the workplace, are to:

- Play harp, flute, or classical music in the background—allow yourself to connect with the music to keep the flow of energy moving through you and to prevent energy from getting stuck
- Breathe—allow your soul to reconnect with the breath of God
- Meditate—take 5-10 minutes to clear your mind
- Take a break and stretch—take time to disconnect and re-center yourself.

Thump the Thymus

… to center yourself and bring you back into balance.

Release Emotional Trauma

Place one hand across your forehead and the other hand across the back of the skull at the nape of the neck (base of the occipital bone). Hold your hands in place while you bring up the trauma to release. Allow your body to release in whatever way it desires.

Your head may go in circles or rock back and forth, lean to the left or lean to the right. You may cry, or your body may tremble. No matter what happens, keep your hands in place and allow the body to release the trauma. You will know you are done when you experience a nice, deep breath (involuntary). It will happen naturally. This is the release to let you know you are done.

You can perform this procedure on other people, especially children.

Talk to Your Body

Everything in life has a consciousness. Talk to your body. Tell it you are grateful for all that it has done for you. Apologize for the trauma you have stored in that body part. Tell the body part it is time to heal, and you wish to help with this healing. Allow yourself to release the stored trauma. See the body part fully healed. Believe the body part is healing and that the healing will be complete one day soon. Anything is possible. The sky's the limit!

Visualization

Visualization is a very powerful tool to bring about healing.

Close your eyes and visualize emerald green healing light coming in through your crown chakra, down into your head, and watch it go through every part of your body, down to your feet. The green light moves through each one of your chakras and out into your energy field. Hold that vision, watching the green healing light move through you to heal and re-energize every part of your being.

Close your eyes and visualize emerald green healing light coming into the afflicted body part. Watch it shrinking. Watch it releasing from the body. See the body part healed. Know it to be true. Do this as often as necessary.

Before going to bed at night, ask your angels and spirit guides to take you to the Jade Temple for healing during your dreamtime.

Three self-healing techniques you can do on yourself are: the Emotional Freedom Technique (EFT), Tapas Acupressure Technique (TAT), and the Emotion Code. Search the Internet for more information on these techniques.

White Dove Circle Energy Blankets

For adults, children, infants, and pets

An energy blanket is a blanket that has been infused with healing energy to provide physical, mental, emotional, and spiritual healing. It is a simple, effective, and powerful method to assist in healing. Using the blanket can help to replenish physical energy and restore mental and emotional clarity and focus. Healing comes faster when a healing blanket is used.

Energy blankets treat the whole person including mind, body, emotions, and spirit. Benefits include: relaxation and feelings of peace, security, and well-being.

Energy blankets work because the healing energy from the blanket flows through the afflicted parts of the energy body, charging them with positive energy. It raises the vibratory level of the energy field in and around the physical body where the negative thoughts and feelings are found. This causes the negative energy to break apart and fall aways, thus allowing the life force to flow in a healthy and natural way.

Use a healing blanket while you sleep to help restore your energy and so you sleep better, feeling totally refreshed when you get up the following morning. Place the energy blanket over an afflicted part of the body to direct healing to that area. Animals also love energy blankets and can benefit from the energy as well. The healing energy never washes or wears out.

Healing blankets are available for purchase in White Dove Circle's Gift Shop or by visiting www.whitedovecircle.org.

White Dove Hand & Body Balm

White Dove Hand & Body Balm has been infused with healing energy to assist in healing the mind, body, emotions, and spirit. The combination of the healing energy and natural ingredients used can create many beneficial healing results.

Applied topically, White Dove Hand and Body Balm can be used for burns, rashes, eczema, dermatitis, rheumatism, psoriasis, diaper rash, dry skin, sunburn, peeling skin, wrinkles, blemishes, wrinkles, chapped lips, soften skin and feet, stretch marks, insect bites, poison ivy, and more. Healing takes less time when the balm is used.

Keep the balm away from heat so it does not melt. It will still work, but the consistency changes and it may become rancid. Some people store the balm in their refrigerator.

Ingredients: Shea butter, grapeseed oil, cocoa butter, lavender and Release™ essential oils. Includes vitamins A, E, and F, which assist in healing and protecting the skin. This balm is not meant to substitute advice provided by your own physician or other medical professional. Keep away from heat.

White Dove Hand & Body Balm is available for purchase in White Dove Circle's Gift Shop or by visiting www.whitedovecircle.org.

APPENDIX

Body Parts and Symptoms, What They Represent Spiritually

The following is an excerpt from the book, *Self-Empowerment: The Only Way to Heal* by Patricia Zimmerman (@ WDC Publishing Co., Inc. All rights reserved.):

Each body part and symptom connected to it functions on a physical level similar to a spiritual level. You will find the metaphors we are so familiar with actually contain truths about our bodies. For example, someone who is a "pain in the neck" can actually become a pain in our neck (the place where we store the emotion). What appears to be merely common sense really makes perfect sense!

Body Parts

Generally speaking, the **right side of the body** represents what is currently taking place in our world, and the **left side of the body** represents the past (including past lives). Though this is true most of the time, the left side can also represent a female or something coming into our lives, while the right side can represent a male or something leaving.

The **adrenal glands** correspond to our "fight or flight" response, which kicks in when we feel threatened or in danger. Problems with the adrenal glands represent issues of trust. Not trusting yourself exhausts the adrenals.

The **arms** symbolize our ability to get "our arms around something" (e.g. to comprehend and embrace a thought, idea, or situation).

The **arteries** and **veins** allow the Light to flow. Hardening of the arteries shuts the flow down. There is no flexibility in life, which leads to chaos.

The **back** is our file drawer. Each vertebra is similar to a file folder. Each file represents a different emotion (e.g., blame, shame, guilt, etc.).

The closer to the neck (the front of the file drawer), the more current the pain. The closer to the coccyx (the back of the file drawer), the more traumatic the pain. We tend to store files we use daily in the front of the file drawer, and traumas we want to bury in the back of the file drawer. The further down we bury the trauma, the harder it is to release. Sometimes it is buried so deeply that we don't even remember it is there.

Birthmarks are where we store trauma from a past life within the physical body. They can also symbolize a time of courage ("badge of honor") from a past life.

The **bladder** is where we store our feelings of being "pissed off" until we can express our anger in words or actions. In other words, we are not speaking our truth. (It's not what you say but how you say it that counts!) Failure to release repressed anger creates disillusionment and lack of self-esteem, which creates dis-ease.

Blood symbolizes our ability to find joy in life. Bad cholesterol symbolizes "clogs" in the joy of life. If we are not in the flow of life, we are not at peace.

Bones are the framework that enables us to experience human form. Physically, bones protect internal organs and provide movement within the body (working together with the skeletal muscles, tendons, ligaments, and cartilage). Spiritually, bones hold our beliefs. Emotionally speaking, the bones are where we experience the feeling of crumbling or falling apart. We feel lost, and then we lose our Light. A fractured bone is the sign of a spirit that is breaking. A broken bone is the sign of a broken spirit. People with these injuries have deep hurts, which go to the core. A broken bone as a result of an accident symbolizes someone with a broken spirit who feels their world is "crashing in" on them.

The **brain** is our computer. Headaches let us know the brain is about to shut down. It is on overload. A migraine will completely shut you down. The brain is a master gland. It is in constant communication with the body, telling it what to do as directed by our thoughts and emotions.

The **cells** are stations for Light in the spirit body. Ideally, these stations will be filled with positive emotions such as trust, love, and joy. A high red blood cell count is a sign of being too grounded in the material world. A high white blood cell count means we desire to be in the spirit realm. We are not grounded. We are escaping lessons we came to learn. Ideally, our red and white blood cells should be in balance. When they are balanced, we are connected to Mother Earth (grounded) and to God.

The **central nervous system** consists of the brain and the spinal cord. The brain contains neurotransmitters that fire and direct information. The amount of electrical impulse determines how the body "lights up" with emotion. The **spinal cord** takes the emotion and sends it to the corresponding organ to be released or stored for use at a later time.

The **ears** symbolize what we hear or don't want to hear. Someone who is born deaf may have chosen to learn to develop their spiritual ears, or their situation may be a way they chose to balance karma from a past life or to teach others.

The **eyes** symbolize how we view life—what we want to see and what we don't want to see in life. Someone who is born blind may have chosen to learn to develop their spiritual eyes, or their situation may be a way they chose to balance karma from a past life or to teach others.

The **face** symbolizes how we present ourselves to the world. People who always present a perfect "picture" of themselves (never a hair out of place) usually have something they don't want people to know. They are not honest with themselves or others. Their inner world is not in balance with their outer world. People who always present a disheveled appearance usually feel "messed up;" they cannot see the beauty within.

The feet are our foundation. They represent who we are and our ability to stand up for ourselves. When we literally drag our feet, we need to ask: "In what area of my life am I figuratively dragging my feet?"

The fingers represent the little details of life when it comes to getting our "arms around something." Each finger represents a different issue: The **thumb** hurts when we worry about someone or something we cannot control, or when our intelligence has been insulted. The

index finger hurts when we have a bruised ego or fear something is going to happen. The **middle finger** hurts when we are angry or we feel like we have been taken advantage of sexually. The **ring finger** hurts when we experience difficulties with loved ones with whom we have a soul contract or when we grieve someone or something that can no longer be. The **little finger** represents painful issues with regard to someone within our family, or when we finally see the truth about something we had refused to see.

The **gall bladder** stores resentment, bitterness, envy, and jealousy.

The **glands** (adrenal, pituitary, salivary, etc.) enable communication. The glands are spiritual organs. They represent our relationship with God. When there is a problem with the glands, there is a problem with our relationship with God. We have shut God out.

Hair symbolizes the spiritual path. Balding is a sign of being too entrenched in the physical world (too materialistic), with little or no connection to the Spirit world. The thinning of hair symbolizes stress, "pulling our hair out" over someone or something.

Hands grasp. The stronger we hold onto something (e.g., a belief, fear, or trauma), the harder it is to let go. Arthritis in the hands represents old, hardened hurts stored there.

The **heart** symbolizes our capacity to give and receive love. Heart dis-ease is the number one killer for men and women in the United States. People with heart problems cannot love themselves. They tend to be rigid, stubborn, and selfish. They lack the capacity for intimacy (when you touch with your hands, you touch with your heart). They work more from their head than they do from the heart. Their love is conditional. People with heart issues hold a lot of loss (e.g., a loved one, a job, etc.). Their heart aches. After grieving, they have trouble moving forward. They lose trust in the process of life. They deny their heart and their spirit because they are not in tune with their heart's desire. Self-worth, self-esteem, and self-love are held in the heart. People with heart issues are stubborn. They have a lot of physical stiffness because they are inflexible in their way of thinking. Love heals all wounds. True forgiveness lies in the heart.

Problems with the **immune system** indicate we have become "stuck." We feel we cannot do anything right. We cannot make a difference. When we constantly say "I remember," we begin to live in the past. This breaks down the immune system. Live in the present, the now. Who you were in the past is not who you are. It only helped to create who you are now.

The **intestine** digests and absorbs. When we have trouble releasing "stuff we no longer need," we have trouble going to the bathroom. Problems with the small intestine symbolize our need to be correct. We call in a second opinion. We build an army to prove we are right. Truth needs no army. People who have trouble making a decision can have problems with the small intestine. Problems with the large intestine symbolize bitterness stored within. We cannot let go of the hurt and the pain. Abandonment issues are held in the large intestine. If you did not have a nurturing relationship with your mother, the trauma will be held here. Constipation symbolizes holding onto negative beliefs and fears. Diarrhea is a sign of self-disgust, self-criticism, self-disappointment, and emotional negativity. Irritable bowel syndrome results from an extreme amount of stress. Diverticulitis symbolizes pockets where old hurts such as blame, shame, and guilt are stored.

Joints (e.g., hips, knees, elbows) are decision-makers. They represent choices in life. Joints move one way or the other (symbolizing choices to be made). We experience pain in a joint when we resist doing what we know we should be doing. What we resist, persists. Continued resistance can wear down the physical body and cause permanent damage.

The **kidneys** (like the bladder) are connected to being "pissed off." They are the control center for guilt. Blame is stored as guilt, as we often blame others for our own mistakes.

The **legs** move us forward in life. When we resist doing what we know we should be doing, we experience pain. When we have trouble standing, it may be because we have trouble standing up for ourselves. When only one leg hurts, it may be because we feel we don't "have a leg to stand on."

Ligaments and tendons are the bands of tissue that connect and hold the muscles and bones together so that they can move within the frame. This is where we feel the burdens of life.

The **liver** holds extreme anger. The skin and eyes turn yellow—jaundice—with liver failure. The color yellow symbolizes cowardliness ("yellow belly"). Life has become too painful. We have made the decision not to move forward in life. It takes courage to move through adversity. It takes courage to look at the self to see what lesson we are learning. It is much easier to blame someone else, especially God, for our problems. We refuse to accept responsibility for what we have created.

The lungs represent our capacity to take in life. Asthma represents not being sure if you want to live or die. You either breathe or you don't. You want to live, or you don't. Grief is held here. Allergies are triggers to past traumas (in the current or a past life).

The **lymph nodes** symbolize our connection with Spirit. When we experience problems here, Spirit is not moving through us. We have become disconnected. We ask, "Why God?" We blame God for something we brought to us as a result of our thoughts, words, and deeds. We refuse to see the truth.

The lymphatic system holds feelings of being walked on or used. People-pleasers experience problems in this area. They want to be the "good guy." If you are always trying to please everyone else, you are "buying" love.

The **mouth** symbolizes the words we speak. Are they kind and loving words, or are they negative and cutting? Are we speaking our truth, or are we holding it in? Anger is stored in the gums (we grit our teeth). It is a "root" emotion (teeth have roots).

The **muscles** permit movement within the temple, allowing balance and harmony to exist. They symbolize power. They move the bones (our beliefs). The stomach and the heart are composed of muscular tissue. Muscle issues symbolize a loss of power, energy, authority, or identity. When we demonstrate extreme power in the physical body (e.g. through excessive muscle building), the spirit inside will feel extremely vulnerable. To maintain peace, our inner world must be in balance with our outer world. Someone who appears to be very weak on the outside does not recognize the power within. Someone who appears to be very strong on the outside is camouflaging the weakness within; e.g., a bully.

The **neck** supports the head. When pain is experienced here, ask yourself: "Who is my pain in the neck?" The neck is also where we store the emotion or experience of having our heads "chopped off" or of being "hung out to dry." Often people who have had their heads chopped off or have been hung in a past life don't like to wear anything around their necks.

We communicate—with ourselves and with others—through our **nerves**. Nerve damage results when we shut down communication with our higher self. We do not want to accept responsibility for what we have created. It is easier to blame someone else (victimhood). We feel "stuck" in a situation for which we don't see a way out. Nerves are slow to heal because we find it difficult to accept responsibility for our role in what happened. We are stuck in blame. Remember, you created your world, and you have the power to change it. Fear is the only thing that stops us.

The **ovaries** are where the eggs are released, allowing for creation of the temple. Cellular memory begins here. All of our memories are held in our energy field and connect to us through the cells. Fears and traumas from past lives are brought in here. Something taking place in the present can trigger a memory from a past life.

The **pancreas** symbolizes the way life treats us. It is where we hold feelings of victimhood (from our current or past lives). It is about making someone else responsible for our actions. Therefore, someone who believes he or she is a victim of life has trouble with his or her pancreas. These people are heavily into blame. They cannot accept responsibility for what they have created in the past (current life or past life). Those with childhood diabetes have been victimized in a past life.

The **prostate** is a gland of the male reproductive system. Its primary function is to secrete an alkaline fluid that nourishes and protects the sperm, an essential part of the process of conception.[103] It is the cellular memory of a trauma that needs to be resolved from a previous lifetime that is carried forward to complete the evolutionary process.

---

[103] https://www.verywellhealth.com/prostate-anatomy-4842562

The **reproductive organs** reproduce situations for lessons to take place. When we have problems with the reproductive organs, we are repeating a lesson from the past or a past life we haven't learned. We are making the same mistake, going into fear instead of love. This system is a highly developed spiritual system. Feelings stored here are lack of desire, pleasure, and frustration. Hatred of men and women can be found here as well. This is where we become "like" mom or dad. Obsessive desires are held here, as well as sexual patterns (extreme sexual acting out) from nymphomania to celibacy. A belief that sex is dirty or sinful is held here.

Respiratory problems are usually found in people who tend to need a lot of attention. They feel helpless and always want to heal someone when, truthfully, they are the ones who need healing most. Subconsciously, they feel if they focus on others, they won't have to look at themselves.

Shoulders are where we carry our burdens, the weight of our world. People who are low on energy have difficulty standing straight. Their shoulders bend forward slightly. Hunched shoulders are a form of protection. We protect the heart because we do not want to get hurt again. It is also a sign of low self-esteem and low self-worth.

Sinuses hold feelings of irritation (often at somebody close to you), abandonment, grief, and withdrawal. The sinuses filter our feelings. How many times do we let the little irritations get "under our skin?"

The **skin** is a filter. It is our protective covering. When working in the negative, it represents self-sabotage or a faulty way of thinking. When we are "thin skinned," we are overly sensitive to criticism. When our skin is too thick. We have become hardened to life, unsympathetic to other people's feelings or circumstances. When this filter is overloaded, it begins throwing everything out: hives (small hidden fears, making a mountain out of a molehill), boils (anger "boiling" over), acne (not liking or accepting the self for who we are or what we have done in the past), eczema (mental outbursts, resentment, bitterness), and psoriasis (afraid of being hurt). Bug bites ask the question, "What's bugging you?" This can explain why some people get bit more by mosquitoes than others.

184

The **spleen** is the organ with the memory of "always remembering the Light within." People with spleen problems feel trapped or closed in. They need to be inspired to help them find their way in life.

The **stomach** symbolizes our ability to digest a thought or idea. This is where we process our feelings and beliefs and how we react to a situation. Nausea and the flu are a result of not being able to "stomach" someone or something. We are "releasing." Perfectionism is held here, blaming someone or something else for things not going the way we thought they should (an expectation or attachment to the outcome).

Teeth symbolize the ability to make decisions. Black teeth are the sign of a perpetual liar (white lies included).

The **testes** are storage units for the sperm, a place of safe-keeping for the cellular memory. The question asked here is: "Will you re-create the same illness/health issue in the body?" Fears and traumas from the past and past lives are brought in here. Something taking place in the present can trigger a memory from a past life. Change the outcome by moving into love.

The **thighs** represent our relationship with our parents and grandparents, especially with the father and grandfather. Old hurts are stored here until we are ready to release them.

The **throat** symbolizes our ability to express ourselves. Are your words filled with anger, criticism, judgment, or blame; or are they kind and loving? Are you speaking your truth, or holding it in? Remember, it's not what you say. It's how you say it that counts. Timing is everything. Sometimes our throats close when we cannot say what we need to say. We feel no one will listen. When your throat hurts during a conversation, it may be because you are not getting your right words out or you may be speaking negatively about someone or something.

The **thymus**, a spiritual organ, represents our sense of hope. If we have a problem with our thymus, we feel a sense of hopelessness (no chance for change).

The **thyroid**, another spiritual organ, promotes energy. It represents taking energy and putting it into manifested form. When energy becomes blocked, we feel unable to communicate what is being said or received. Severe energy loss and metabolic changes (hyper or hypo) are symptoms of a weakened thyroid. Trauma and fear created by religion are held here (e.g., hell and brimstone, fire and damnation, a God we must fear). The thyroid represents our relationship with our earthly father and how we learn about our spiritual father from him.

The **uterus** is where the temple is constructed and protected. Cellular memory begins to take on form and remembers patterns here.

Spiritual Dis-eases

The following is an excerpt from the book, *Self-Empowerment: The Only Way to Heal* by Patricia Zimmerman (@ WDC Publishing Co., Inc. All rights reserved.):

You will never understand the world around you until you understand the world within. There are some "dis-eases" which researchers will never find a cure, no matter how hard they try, because the root cannot be found in the physical. It is spiritual. Some of these "dis-eases" include:

Sudden Infant Death Syndrome (SIDS) to this day is still unexplained. No matter how much research is done to find a cure, it will never be found because the root of the dis-ease is spiritual.

SIDS takes place when the incarnating soul changes its mind and decides to go back Home. An incoming spirit has up to two years to change its mind, hence the soft spot on the baby's head. This soft spot is where the spirit enters and leaves the body. Once the spot has closed, the spirit must live the life it has chosen. The spirit can come and go temporarily through the solar plexus (also known as "the seat of the soul") when the body is at rest.

We came from the spirit side where we were nothing but pure Light. We had no dense physical body. During pregnancy, the spirit will enter and leave the body of the fetus so it can get used to being in a dense, physical body once more. For a spirit to stay in a body for nine months straight is similar to being imprisoned, a cruel and unjust punishment.

During pregnancy, the spirit goes in and out, charting its life, getting used to the denseness of the physical body, and letting the parents know what it wants for a name, as well as its likes and dislikes. Why do you think parents say, "No, that doesn't feel right," or "That's not it" when naming their child? They are intuiting the child's name.

The child's name and date of birth (numerology) are important. Together they create an energetic road map of their purpose for coming into life, their personality, their destiny, and much more.

The flutter or movement an expectant mother feels is the spirit present in the physical body. The spirit comes and goes but does not fully enter the physical body until two days before to two days after birth.

Upon entering life, a spirit can still change its mind for various reasons, including:

- The circumstances were not right for its spiritual evolution.
- The mother may not have been ready to have a child, and the child recognized this.
- The child did not feel loved.
- The child got homesick and decided to go Home. Remember, they just came from God where there is nothing but pure love.

It is extremely important for an infant to feel loved. The human touch is a powerful tool to express love. Babies need to be held and cuddled. They need to be talked to and to feel loved.

Typically, we surround little girls with pink (the color of love) and little boys with blue (the color of Spirit). The more we use the color blue when decorating a child's room or dressing them, the more homesick the child can become. It is better to use the colors pink (love), green (healing), purple (the Divine), or yellow (intellect) to welcome a child into life. Use the color blue sparingly.

Babies are more sensitive than we realize. They feel different levels of energy better than most adults. Babies can sense the difference between the energy of love and that of fear.

Fear to an infant feels like pins and needles. This explains why a baby will cry for no apparent reason when someone who is fearful holds them or when they are in an environment full of negativity.

Scoliosis occurs after the age of ten. From a spiritual perspective, we get our "karmic package" between the ages of nine and fourteen. Because we cannot possibly balance all our karma in one lifetime, we choose to balance karma from three to four lifetimes during an incarnation.

This explains the hormonal changes at the time of puberty; something feels different. Young adults don't know who they are anymore, and they do not like who they once were (acne) on a subconscious level.

The karmic package comes in the form of a ball of energy. When "opened," the ball of energy disseminates into the body's energy field to be balanced at a later date.

The spirit receiving the karmic package may think, "Life is good. Why open it now and ruin everything?" If the spirit refuses to "open" the package, the spirit pushes the package "to the back" so it doesn't have to look at it, and there it will stay until the spirit decides to accept responsibility for what it once created.

The spine was made to be flexible, and this flexibility includes the ability to wrap around a ball of energy (even if we do not see it). When the karmic package is pushed to the back, the vertebrae begin to wrap around the ball, resulting in curvature of the spine.

The sooner the karmic package is opened, while the bones are still flexible, the sooner the spine will straighten. If we wait too long, the bones become hardened or "set" because we have become inflexible or "set" in our way of thinking.

Once the karmic package is opened and the spirit accepts responsibility for what they once did, the energy will disseminate into the energy field and the spine will automatically straighten—without surgery.

Physical challenges, such as being disabled, disfigured, or deformed, are chosen for soul growth. They can be a humbling experience. You are forced to look at yourself for who you really are—not who others thought you were. You learn not to take on other people's fears when ridiculed. This is their lesson—not yours. You learn that you are not your physical body. You are the beautiful soul that lives within the body. Your lesson is to learn to love and accept the beautiful soul you are.

Physical challenges teach you to strive for greater heights as you struggle to overcome your limitations instead of allowing others to do things for you. You learn to accept or reject parts of yourself and others. You gain understanding. You learn not to judge others. The karma being balanced can equal ten or more lifetimes.

You learn not to take people and life for granted as you gain an appreciation for the lessons and blessings of life. A special blessing is received when you draw on your inner strength and use it to help others based on what you have learned from your experiences.

Alzheimer's is another misunderstood phenomenon. Researchers will never find a cure for this condition because it is a spiritual gift.

Alzheimer's takes place when the spirit no longer desires to be in the physical body. This person has lost their desire to live. The spirit wants to go Home, but the physical body can still be used for others (such as family, friends, doctors, nurses, etc.) to work out karma so the spirit of the loved one leaves the physical body slowly to make it easier for the family to let him or her go.

People with Alzheimer's revert back in time. They remember better times, re-living those moments in their mind. Soon they mentally become the age they were in their memories, remembering only the good times. When challenges are remembered, they go back even farther in time. They go back, farther and farther, until they become like babies who must be spoon fed. Eventually they go back into the womb and forget how to swallow (they didn't have to swallow in the womb).

If you want to help loved ones so they do not draw Alzheimer's to them, help them to stay focused on the present and the future, never the past. People who live in the past have lost their desire to live. They have no purpose. They feel stuck and see no way out so they slowly begin to withdraw from life.

Sometimes, towards the end of the dis-ease, another spirit roaming the astral realm may take over the body. This would explain why some Alzheimer's patients do things they would never have dreamt of doing. For example, someone who spent a life being prudish now runs around naked. The loved one's spirit is no longer present.

Women with **menstruation problems**, such as heavy bleeding, often have experienced trauma in a past life and have brought that emotion in with them.

Years ago, a friend of mine in her mid-50s suffered from intense cramping, swollen breasts, and heavy bleeding during her menstrual cycle long after menopause. This cramping felt like labor pains.

During a past-life regression, we learned my friend was a slave in the south (United States). Her owner had impregnated her because her skin was light in color and his wife couldn't bear children. The baby was to go to the slave owner's wife at birth so she would have a child of her own.

The owner and his wife arrived when it was time to deliver the baby. My friend screamed repeatedly, "Please don't take my baby. Please don't take my baby." Unbeknownst to the wife, my friend and the slave owner had a secret relationship. This baby was a part of him that belonged to her—not his wife. My friend couldn't bear the thought of losing the baby. She died in childbirth, a result of hemorrhaging.

When I put my hands on my friend's pelvic area to send healing energy, my friend began to scream with labor pains, picking up where she once left off. The excessive bleeding and pain she experienced monthly since a teenager was her subconscious mind trying to deliver the baby from this past life. We "pretended" to deliver the baby. My friend pushed and I coached until the baby arrived. I cleaned the baby up, then placed the baby on her chest. My friend said she could feel the baby's breath. Her soul was now at peace.

My friend was black in this past life and white in the present life. I have friends who are black now and were white in a past life. As part of our Earthly experience, we live and experience in different races, cultures, and religions because they all contribute to our learning and spiritual growth. Never be prejudiced against anyone because sooner or later, in one of your many future lives, you can be guaranteed you will be on the opposite end of what you once gave out (karma).

It doesn't matter who you once were. What matters is who you are now and how you live your present life. Your past lives helped to create the person you are now. Leave the past behind where it belongs. We only visit the past to gain knowledge and for healing. Heal the past to heal the present.

Women who can't get pregnant often unconsciously blame themselves for losing a baby in a past life. They do not feel worthy of bringing a child into life because of what happened in the past. This happens quite often, and a past-life regression can help to heal the wound so the young woman can get pregnant.

Once the young woman realizes the baby's death was not her fault, she can forgive herself. When blame and guilt are released, pregnancy is just around the corner. Subsequent pregnancies take place without complications.

It is important to remember we choose how and when we will die before incarnating. This means we can choose to die as an infant, a child, a teenager, or as an adult. Once our chart has been completed, we go Home. Death is always the soul's choice (free will).

Children who die young or as an infant came in with the specific purpose to help loved ones open their hearts to love and to teach love is the only thing that matters. Quite often, parents are too focused on the material world and have forgotten the spiritual world. If the death of the child makes us bitter, our hearts close. We wallow in our own misery (self-pity), and we never see the beauty of the gift. Out of every "bad" situation in life comes something beautiful.

For example, a tornado that tears through a downtrodden town will most often pull the town back together as the town works to clean up the mess left behind by the tornado. That which was once destroyed is rebuilt, bringing new life to the area. If the work is done, the town will be in much better shape than it was before the tornado hit. If the work is not done, the town will never recover.

Some women choose not to have children to learn to be independent. For example, a friend of mine, as a young girl, told her mother "she chose not have children in this lifetime." My friend had experienced a dis-ease in a past life that made her dependent on others. In this life, she chose to learn to be independent.

Some women may not have been good mothers in a past life and choose to observe how to be a good mother in this life. The body may have been designed to keep the mother from getting pregnant to fulfill her life lesson.

There are many different reasons why a woman cannot get pregnant, and they are all spiritual.

Abortion within the first trimester is not as terrible as religion makes it out to be. The incarnating soul is aware of the young woman's state of mind. It knows she is not ready to be a mother. Since the soul does not enter the physical body until right around the time of birth, the soul would not be in the body when the fetus was aborted. You can kill the body, but you can never kill the soul.

A client of mine never told anyone, not even her parents or her husband, she'd had an abortion as a teenager. She had trouble getting pregnant because she felt guilty for having had the abortion. Eventually my client got pregnant, and when her daughter was around the age of four, she looked up at her mother and said, "It's okay if you weren't ready for me before, mommy. I'm here now." True story.

Remember, your physical body is the vehicle your spirit chose to drive around in life. The driver of a car usually does not take possession of the car until right before or after it comes off the production line.

Adopted children always wind up with the parents they were supposed to be with for their spiritual evolution. The birth mother was only the vehicle for the child to come through to get to its intended parents.

When a **child is born out of wedlock**, there is usually a soul contract between the two parents to bring that child into the world (including one-night stands). The incoming child required both parents for its character traits and genes to create the physical body. Once the soul contract is complete, the parents can decide whether or not to stay together.

Death can be difficult to understand when one is not on the spiritual path. We fear the unknown of what comes next for the dying person and for us.

Souls leave the earth plane in many different ways. Death can be expected or unexpected. It is easier to let go of someone who has been very sick because you don't want them to suffer. It is much harder to let go of someone who dies unexpectedly.

A group of people leaving the earth plane together (e.g., a plane crash or an accident) chose to die together before incarnating. Their death usually brings about change.

There are as many ways to die as there are reasons for dying. How one dies is a personal choice made before incarnating into a life.

When someone you love is dying, love him or her enough to let them go. Hanging onto a loved one serves no purpose. Allowing them to suffer because of your own personal needs is selfish.

Letting a loved one go when it is time will not only help you with your healing, it will help your loved one in his or her next life, too.

How to Care for Your Fourfold Being

The following should be done daily to maintain a high vibration and a healthy fourfold body:

Spiritual
- Meditate
  - ten minutes every day, eyes open, to align your fourfold being
  - fifteen minutes longer as time permits (after ten minutes with eyes open), eyes closed, to go deeper
- Personal prayers
  - Ask so you can receive. Pray out loud so the Universe can hear you.
  - Give gratitude. It is the highest vibrational form of prayer there is.
- Recite I Am Decrees
- Begin your day by taking three to four nice, deep cleansing breaths to release stress—in through the nose, out through the mouth. Then say: *I Am beautiful! I Am beautiful! I Am beautiful! And I Am ready for a wonderful day. I Am ready to give all that I can and receive all that I can.*
- Have confidence in knowing you are never alone, never separate from God.
- Remember, love is the key to fighting off anything negative spiritually.

Mental
- You are a Creator. There is nothing you cannot do if you have a heartfelt desire to obtain it.
- Keep your thoughts positive and loving. Always look at the bright side for all things change.

- Low vibrational thoughts and feelings come from low vibrational angels. When negative thoughts arise, spend three to five minutes by giving gratitude or saying I Am decrees to push them away.
- Apologize when appropriate, even when your mental says you should not.
- Seek Truth always! Question, question, question everything so that you will know Truth.
- Read high vibrational spiritual information daily.
- Sharpen your brain every day through games, puzzles, and conversation.

Emotional

- Stay away from energy vampires.
  - Do not try to rescue them or reinforce their negative behaviors in any manner.
  - Limit eye contact with them. Eyes are the entranceway to the soul. Protect your soul. Say: *In the name of All There Is, Was, and Ever Shall Be, I bring about a covering of light and love to shield me from all harm, especially any penetration of my auric field of energy. This is for my highest good. So it is uttered. So it is done.*
- Be compassionate with others. Have compassion for yourself.
- Keep in mind each of us on Earth behaves as we do, or have, contingent upon the information we have received and accepted at the vibration that we may be at the time.
- Continually check to make sure your thoughts, words, beliefs, and actions are positive, loving, and truthful.
- Write release letters, whenever appropriate.
- Be the peace you wish to see in this world.
- Stay humble. If you don't, the ego (Edging God Out) will gladly provide a very tough lesson for you to learn.
- Have hope! Trust in the process of life. There is reason and purpose for everything.

Physical

Take the appropriate vitamins and supplements for your height, weight, and skeletal frame. Your daily multivitamin should include:

- Vitamin D
- Magnesium
- Calcium
- Zinc
- Iron
- Folate (folic acid)
- Vitamin B-12

- Meals should consist of small portions versus larger portions. While meat can be eaten, a plant-based diet is best for your body physically and spiritually.
- Juice (smoothies)—to give your body the vitamins, minerals, and nutrients it needs.
- Exercise for your height, weight, and skeletal frame. Make sure a cardiovascular component is included to ensure the proper oxygenation and blood flow are occurring within your being.
- Walk 10,000 steps each day.
- Do not fall for fads that spring from greed. You are similar, yet different, from everyone else.

Acid-Forming and Alkaline-Forming Foods

Taken from the Edgar Cayce Health Database
http://www.edgarcayce.org/are/holistic_health/data/thdiet3.html

Edgar Cayce recommended a diet that is 80 percent alkaline to 20 percent acid. It should be noted that because a food is acid is no indication that it REMAINS acid in the body. It can turn alkaline. Honey and raw sugars produce alkaline ash, but because of a high concentrate of sugar become acid-formers. Those fruits marked with an * should not be eaten with other foods. They are acid externally but alkaline internally. Listed below is a list of foods that are alkaline or acidic in their reaction:

Alkaline Fruits	Acid Fruits	Alkaline Vegetables	Acid Vegetables
Apples/cider	All preserves	Alfalfa sprouts	Asparagus tips
Apricots	All canned with	Artichokes	(white only)
Avocados	sugar	Asparagus	Beans (dried)
Bananas	Blueberries	Bamboo shoots	Garbanzos
Berries (most)	Cranberries	Beans (green,	Lentils
Cantaloupe	Dried-sulphured,	lima, wax,	
Carob (pod	glazed	string)	
only)	Olives	Beets	
Cherries	(Pickled)	Broccoli	
Citron	Plums	Cabbages	
Currants	Prunes	Carrots	
Dates		Celery	
Figs		Cauliflower	
Grapes		Chard	
*Grapefruit		Chicory	
Guavas		Corn	
*Kumquats		Cucumber	
*Lemons (ripe)		Dill	
*Limes			

Loquats		Dock	
Mangos		Dulse	
Nectarines		Eggplant	
Olives (ripe)		Endive	
*Oranges		Escarole	
Papayas		Garlic	
Passion Fruit		Horseradish	
Peaches		Jerusalem	
Pears		artichokes	
Persimmons		Kale	
Pineapple		Leeks	
(fresh)		Lettuce	
Pomegranates		Mushrooms	
Melons (all)		Okra	
Raisins		Onions	
Sapotes		Oyster plant	
Tamarind		Parsley	
*Tangerines		Parsnips	
Tomatoes (fully		Peas	
ripened)		Peppers (bell)	
		Potatoes (skin	
		is best	
		part)	
		Pumpkin	
		Radish	
		Romaine	
		lettuce	
		Rutabagas	
		Sauerkraut	
		Soybeans	
		Spinach	
		Sprouts	
		Squash	
		Turnips	
		Watercress	
		Yams, sweet	
		potatoes	

Alkaline Dairy	Acid Dairy		

Acidophilus milk
Buttermilk
Milk (raw only—
   human, cow, or
goat)
Whey
Yogurt
	Butter
	Cheese (all)
	Cottage cheese
	Cream
	Custards
	Margarine
	Milk (boiled,
	cooked,
	   malted, dried,
	   canned)		

Alkaline Grains	Acid Grains	Alkaline, Misc.	Acid, Misc.

Amaranth
Quinoa
Buckwheat &
millet are
   thought to be
either   neutral or
alkaline.
	All grains and grain
	   products except
	   buckwheat &
	millet
		Agar
		Coffee
		substitute
		Honey
		Kelp (edible)
		Tea (herbal
		& Chinese)
		Egg yolks
			Alcoholic
			drinks
			Cocoa
			Coffee, Indian
			teas
			Condiments
			(all)
			Dressings
			Drugs
			Eggs (whites)
			Flavorings
			Mayonnaise
			Tapioca
			Tobacco
			Vinegar

Alkaline Nuts	Acid Nuts	Alkaline Flesh Food	Acid Flesh Food
Almonds Chestnuts (roasted) Coconut (fresh)	All except above Coconut (dried)	Beef Juice Blood & bone (only bonemeal is alkaline)	All meats Fowl, fish, shellfish Gelatin

Note: The above information is not intended for self-diagnosis or self-treatment. Please consult a qualified health care professional for

assistance in applying the information contained in the Cayce Health
Database.

Essential Oils for Healing

The following is an excerpt from the book, *The Sapiential Discourses: Universal Wisdom, Book IV, Spiritual Warfare*, by All There Is, Was, and Ever Shall Be through Elliott Eli Jackson, pp.158-160

All of you on Earth should at least have the following. Period.

Release to send away pain and discomfort, as well as lower portions of US from your being, household, or anything else

Thieves, Lemon, Eucalyptus, Rosemary, Clove – to be used as an antiseptic, mouthwash, cleaners, and for use in pain relief

Lavender to be used for burns, calming, bruises, and skin irritations

Peppermint to be used for headaches, pain, and itching

Wintergreen to be used for pain relief in bones, muscles, and joints

Frankincense, Blue Cypress, Sandalwood to be used to stimulate limbic portion of the brain and relieve depression; also good for grounding yourself and other things

Sage to be used for clearing and cleansing, purifying, pushing away unwanted/unneeded lower portions of US from any place; may also be used for oral infections and certain skin conditions

Spearmint, Patchouli to be used as digestive aids

Spikenard use for any circulation issues

Patchouli can be used as an anti-inflammatory and to prevent wrinkles, chapped skin; also stops itching

Ginger to be used for the respiratory, infections, pain, nausea, sex drive, and as an expectorant

Cypress – to be used to aid circulation and opens blood capillaries

Roman Chamomile – to be used for nerve regeneration, toothaches, issues with liver, and to detoxify the blood

Clove to be used as a mental stimulant and helps with sleep, toothaches, acne, ulcers, hepatitis, and to rid the body of intestinal parasites

Hyssop to be used for the respiratory infections, worms; can assist your meditative process (place on temples)

Jasmine can be used as a fragrance, antidepressant, all menstrual problems, and other female issues

Lemongrass can help with lymph flow; also an antiparasitic

Rose may be used to reduce scarring, for anxiety, skin conditions, and as a fragrance

Thyme may be used as an anti-aging agent and to slow Alzheimer's

Crystals That Assist in Releasing Cancer

~ All There Is, Was, and Ever Shall Be through Elliott Eli Jackson

Bix Bite (aka, Red Beryl)—Key words: vitality, courage, love, self-esteem and passion. AKA Red Beryl stimulates courage, passion, vitality, strength of purpose. It can help revitalize people who are fatigued, stressed or convalescing after a long illness. It supports the body's ability to repair itself.

Clinochlore—Key Words: Healing, vitality, love, the Divine blueprint of well-being, angelic communication. Clinochlore minerals have extensive healing properties. They are one of the strongest mineral groups to use for support in healing cancer.

Elestial Quartz—Key Words: Energy infusion from the higher realms, Divine love, angelic communication, grounding. Elestial Quartz are excellent healing tools for skeletal issues. They are also excellent in recovery from bone cancers.

Epidote—Key Words: Release of negativity, embracing positive patterns, attraction of what one emanates. Epidote is excellent for physical healing. It aids in dissolving blockages, cancerous tumors, cysts, and other manifestations of energetic density.

Galena—Key Words: Shamanic soul retrieval, alchemical self-transformation. Galena is an excellent stone for countering infection. It also helps protect one against the adverse affects of certain types of radiation. Galena is excellent for support in dealing with cancer, particularly where infection is a possibility as a result of chemotherapy or radiation.

Unakite Jasper—Key Words: Healing, balance, release of bad habits, higher attunement. Jasper is a stone of physical strength and energy. It supports in the treatment of cancers or heart disease.

Lemurian Jade (aka, Black Jade)—Key Words: Protection, clearing negativity. Lemurian Jade acts like an spirit 'bodyguard' when it is worn or carried. It is as if the stone makes one 'invisible' to lower vibrations or negative entities and energy vampires. It assists with ridding fear, envy, and doubt.

Snowflake Obsidian—Key Words: Perseverance, insight, attunement to spiritual guidance, past-life recall, spirit communication. Snowflake Obsidian carries courage and persistence to those on the edge of hope. It can also help energetically to limit the spread of cancer cells through the body. It assists one in becoming more receptive to healing energy and a healing attitude.

Prophecy Stone—Key Words: Grounding spiritual light in the physical self and the world, seeing prophetic visions. They are excellent tools for releasing cellular toxins and can help support the body through chemotherapy and radiation to help slow the spread of cancers.

Pyromorphite—Key Words: Enhanced digestion and assimilation, discharge of toxic substances and energies, blending love and will. Pyromorphite is a premier ally for vibrationally regulating the growth of cancer cells and for preventing the spread of cancer to other cells. It can help the body recover more quickly from chemo and radiation.

Seraphinite—Key Words: Self-healing, regeneration, wholeness, angelic connection. Seraphinite can be used to help regulate growth and reproduction of all types of cancerous cells.

Green Tourmaline—Key Words: Healing, strength, vitality, wholeness. Stimulates proper cell function and reproduction. Assists in spiritually treating cancers and cell-growth imbalances.

Malachite—Key Words: Enlightened leadership, creativity, confidence, protection, healed heart. It can assist in restoring strength and vitality after illness and draws toxins from the body. It's excellent for reducing inflammation and detoxification.

Release Letters

Release letters are effective tools for healing because they are symbolic.

- Write the letter to get all of our stored emotions out. You'll be surprised how much comes out when you start writing!
- Tear the letter up (symbolizing the end of the contract).
- Burn the letter (symbolizing the purification taking effect within you).
- Say a prayer (asking for help in transmuting the energy).
- Throw the ashes (symbolizing the release within).

Write a letter to someone else first, then for yourself. You will be amazed at how powerful these letters can be!

Release Letter to Someone Else

Write a letter to whomever you need to release or to whom you must apologize. Be sincere. If the letter is not written from the heart, nothing will change. Do not write the letter if you still hold a grudge against someone. Your intention must be pure.

This is a wonderful tool to release old emotions (current and past lives). Write anything you would like to say. You can even swear. The important thing is to get "stuck" negative thoughts and emotions out so you can be at peace. For example, you can say: "You hurt me when …" "Why did you do that? What were you trying to prove?" "How could you do that to me? You really hurt me." "That was dumb! What were you thinking?!"

Release this person who has hurt you, intentionally or unintentionally, all the way back to the root where the problem began (this is very important!). Heal the past to heal the present. When looking at the weed on top of the ground (current life), you do not see the roots hidden beneath the ground (past lives).

Apologize for anything you may have done to hurt this person, intentionally or unintentionally, in your many lifetimes together (current and past). Most likely, you both have contributed to the problem in one lifetime or another, and that is why you are together now. Unresolved issues keep us tied together throughout eternity until they are resolved.

Send love to this person—all the way back to the root life. At the end of the letter, include this statement: "I love you very much, and I apologize for not accepting you exactly as you are."

You may also add: "Thank you for the gifts we've shared for they have helped to make me the beautiful man/woman that I Am." Or "I fully and completely release you now." (Use this verbiage only if the person you are releasing has died or you never wish to see them again. Never use this verbiage if the person you are releasing is the father/mother of your children and only if they are deceased. Your children still need both parents, not just one. If you use this verbiage in your release letter inappropriately, your child/children will never see their parent again, and this will become karmic for you.)

Take your letter to a place that is sacred to you and to God, and then read it out loud.

Tear the letter up, then burn it, making sure every last piece of paper is burnt. You don't want to leave anything behind.

Now take the ashes outside and say: "Dear God, this has been a burden I no longer wish to carry. Please resolve this for me. Gratitude."

Toss the ashes into the wind.

Release Letter to Yourself

Write a letter to yourself, writing from the heart. This is a wonderful tool to release old stuck emotions (current and past lives). Write anything you would like to say to yourself. You can even swear, if so desired. The important thing is to get "stuck" negative thoughts and emotions out so you can be at peace. When you have peace within, there is peace in your world.

In the letter, you can say anything you want. For example, you can ask yourself: "Why did you say/do that?" "That was dumb! What were you thinking?!" "Why did you make that decision about that job?" "Why do you keep falling into the same old trap?"

Be sure to address any fears you may have that you are ready to release, anything you don't like about yourself, and any problems you may have with someone else (they are a mirror back to you).

Release yourself for whatever you feel you may have done wrong (e.g., for being too judgmental or critical of yourself, for doubting yourself, for not loving yourself, etc.).

Release yourself for not accepting you for who you really are—a work in progress. (We strive for perfection, but we are not there yet!)

And be sure to send love to yourself.

At the end of the letter, include this statement: "I love you very much, and I release you. I apologize for not accepting you exactly as you are."

Take your letter to a place that is sacred to you and to God, and then read it out loud.

Tear the letter up, then burn it, making sure every last piece of paper is burnt. You don't want to leave anything behind.

Now take the ashes outside and say:

"Dear God, this has been a burden I no longer wish to carry. Please resolve it for me. Gratitude."

Toss the ashes into the wind. You will feel different!

Release Letter to Release a Past Life

Write a letter to whatever lifetime that needs to be released. Be sincere. If the letter is not written from the heart, nothing will change. Your intention must be pure.

A release letter is a wonderful tool to release old emotions, vows, and promises (current and past lives). Write whatever you would like to say. The important thing is to get "stuck" negative thoughts and emotions out so your soul can be at peace.

Release this lifetime where you were feeling hurt or abandoned, intentionally or unintentionally, all the way back to the root where it began (very important!). Heal the past to heal the present.

Apologize for anything you may have done to hurt anyone in that lifetime, intentionally or unintentionally. Unresolved issues keep us tied together throughout eternity until they are resolved.

At the end of the letter, include this statement: "I fully and completely release this lifetime and any other lifetime that is keeping me from moving forward in life. I am ready to release that which has been keeping me from becoming my fullest potential."

Releasing Emotional Trauma

Set your intention to "release anything and everything from past lives, present life, and future lives—going back to the root wherever it started—that is causing …"

Then place one hand across the person's (or yours) forehead and the other hand across the back of the skull (base of the occipital bone) at the nape of the neck. Hold hands there for a few minutes while you bring up the memories of the trauma to release. Allow your body to release until you experience a nice, deep breath.

The person's head (or yours) may go in circles, or it may rock back and forth. This is okay. Allow your body to do whatever it is it wants to do. What you are doing is release the trauma from the physical body at the same time you release it from the spirit body.

Keep your hands on the person's (your) head and allow the head to unwind the trauma. You'll know the trauma was released when you involuntarily experience a nice, deep breath. This involuntary release will happen naturally; don't force it.

Do this for three to five minutes. You are peeling "back layers of an onion." Sometimes you can get it all at once; sometimes you need to do it several times before you've released everything.

You can also place two drops each of Release into the palm of your hands, then rub your hands together so the oils get into your hands. Taking deep breaths, breathe in the energy three times. Then do the trauma release. Using Release will help you release whatever it is you no longer need.

About White Dove Circle of Light and Love

White Dove Circle of Light and Love is a non-profit (501c3) spiritual organization. We are:
- a community where people come together,
- a place where you are loved and supported,
- a space where you are free to be who you really are,
- at a time when your spirit needs it most.

White Dove Circle is a unique, one-of-a-kind wellness center where one can find true healing for the mind, body, emotions, and spirit.

White Dove Circle is a leader in the wholistic field offering a wide variety of services and products to heal naturally. We offer 150+ classes, workshops, and retreats for self-improvement and self-empowerment.

Step into our beautiful wellness center and you immediately feel a sense of calm, a sense of peace. You know that where you are is where you're supposed to be!

White Dove Circle offers many opportunities for healing and personal growth:

- *Wellness Center* ~ White Dove Circle's effective and experienced healing practitioners can assist in releasing stress, energizing the body, and in healing the physical body. Maintain health and well-being naturally through energy healing, sound healing, crystal healing, vibrational healing, and more. Pet healing and animal communication are also available at the wellness center.

- *Wellness Clinic* ~ Your first session is free at the Wellness Clinic. Sessions are also free for those who truly cannot afford healing during Wellness Clinic hours. Healing should be for everyone, not just those who can afford it. Come sample what true healing is all about!

- *Classes, Workshops, and Retreats* ~ The physical teacher brings the *student* to the awareness that the most important teacher lies within. One way to define spiritual growth is how you view life and heal when a major change has taken place within your life. Join us for classes, workshops, and retreats for self-improvement and self-empowerment, health and well-being, true healing, meditation, intuitive development, metaphysics, sacred teachings, and more.

- *Advanced Course of Study* ~ A life coach / wellness advocate is someone who helps people move forward in life by setting goals that will help them achieve the life they desire. Our goal is to train knowledgeable, competent coaches who desire to be in service to humanity.

- *Meditation* ~ Silent, guided, salt cave, and crystal bowl meditations are offered to release stress, slow the mind, and find inner peace.

- *Movement Exercises* ~ Movement exercises help to lower blood pressure and reduce insomnia, lessen chronic pain while at the same time improving mobility, flexibility, and strength.

- *Gift Shop and Online Retail Store* ~ Purchase items that support healing and books to assist you on your spiritual journey. Therapeutic essential oils, herbs and supplements, crystals, blankets and balm, and other items that support health and well-being are sold in our Gift Shop or by accessing our online retail store (coming soon!).

Let us assist you on your journey back to a better you.
Come share your heart with us!

TESTIMONIALS

The following testimonials are from clients/guests of White Dove Circle who have experienced true healing from our all-natural types of services and products, whether it be different forms of energy healing or products infused with energy healing. While we have many received many testimonials over the years, only a few were used in this book.

Science has proven we are all energy. Why not use energy to heal energy?! Love and fear are both energies. How we use the energy is up to us.

As stated earlier, the most important thing we can do to release cancer or any other dis-ease is to release fear. The more we fear something we don't want, the more we create it. Focus on what you want, not what you don't want.

Heal the mind, body, and spirit so the physical body can heal.

Cancer Released

"My name is Annie, and I am 73 years old. I have lived most of my life without disease, except for type 2 diabetes. In May of 2022, I was diagnosed with CML Leukemia. In the beginning, I could not walk 20 feet. I had chairs throughout the yard. I was ready to check out!! My friend suggested I sign up for the crystal bed therapy at the White Dove Circle. It was for 5 weeks, twice a week for an hour each session, and it was a 45-minute drive each way to the Center. My first session on the Crystal Bed was November 17, 2022, and by December 16, 2022, my marker numbers were normal.

"After 3½ weeks of the Crystal Bed therapy, I had a life-changing dream. I was riding a chestnut-colored horse with the wind in my hair. It was so real I felt complete joy. I woke up and thought, "I feel healed!" It was amazing! The feeling did not go away. I had a doctor's appointment soon after and told my doctor that I knew I was in remission and told him about the crystal bed. He did not balk and said, "There is a lot we don't know." He said, "So let's check." Yep! I was in remission. I read the book. "You Can Heal Your Life" by Louise Hay, which my friend gave me. I read every page and did exactly what

Louise Hay said, always chanting, "Thank you for my healing," hundreds of times a day and always while on the crystal bed.

"I am still in remission 1½ years later. I am still on chemo pills for now and can recheck my numbers at 2 years, and I may be off meds for the rest of my life. Going to the White Dove Circle saved my life. But you must believe!" ~ A.K., OH

NOTE: Annie is cancer free for more than two years now.

"To all those I love: For over 6 years, I have been battling bilateral breast cancer naturally. It has been quite a journey. I had been given a devastating prognosis, listened to all kinds of advice, even warnings of my ruining my chances of survival by not following protocol. I listened to my higher self, and so far, I am still here. It may not be the chosen path for everyone with cancer, but I truly believe I would not still be here if I agreed to letting them "cut, burn, and poison" the cancer. I never stopped believing I could heal with the right plan!

"Everyone has to follow their own beliefs and their own path. My body is actually healing more every single day, with a little fine tuning and advice from this dedicated person, Pat. My blood work is that of a 17-year-old, and the one tumor I had left is shrinking. I believe in Miracles. This plan has assisted my body to Heal itself, given a little fine tuning.

"There is no actual CURE for CANCER. It is a HEALING. No one can do this for you. You have to do the work to make it happen. You have to BELIEVE, and keep focused, and know that you are worth it, and you are LOVED. ♡♡♡♡" ~ L.G., Estero, FL

"On July 30, 2024, I was diagnosed with Breast C. Everything had changed for me in that second. I felt hopeless no matter what was said to me. Visiting the oncologist, I felt rushed and pressured. That overwhelming feeling put me in a dark place. They were immediately trying to put me on chemotherapy and wanting me to make life changing decisions right then and there. My spirit didn't feel right about it. I felt like a pin cushion and still was in pain from the biopsies and mammograms. One of my spiritual advisors had suggested for me

to get a consultation with Ms. Pat. I called and she got me in the next day. When I walked in the store I felt peace immediately. She greeted me with LOVE. She advised I give her 6 weeks and pause on the hospitals. I'm now focusing on healing my spirit, mental and emotional body first. She provided a guide for me and it's my job to do the work. My friends have noticed my spirit being lifted, and I'm only in the beginning of my journey. I can't wait until I finish my 6-week plan to see my progress. Thank you for your knowledge and pure kindness."
~ D.M., OH

White Dove Circle of Light and Love
dba, White Dove Wellness Center

"White Dove is one of the most healing and wonderful places I have ever stepped foot in. I live about 600 miles away, but I plan on returning many times in the future. The practitioners there have so many amazing gifts. I've had the chance to experience Reiki, the Salt Cave, Crystal Bowl Sound Healing, Soul Connecting, talks, and meditations. I also participate in some of their classes on Zoom occasionally. I can't wait to experience more of the awesome services. Thank you, Pat, and all the other people there for making it the magical place that it is." ~ D.L., NJ

"Life has been so hard since birth. I became so used to pain and darkness, I didn't know that there is light and love. I didn't think I was worthy of anything good. I had to truly suffer and when it got so bad where I was ready to give up, is when I woke up. I still have my ups and downs but I have come a long way these past three years and feel more at peace with who I am. I want to learn so much more about the unseen, how to can heal myself and help others on their journey. I will never forget the pain I had to endure, it is my reminder to give of myself to others so that they don't have to suffer like I did. I can look back now and accept my life, each experience and person has helped me become who I am today and I thank them, forgive and release them and myself. I know now we all play our 'roles' in this incarnation. "I have prayed so hard and asked the Universe to take my hand and light the path for me so that I can find myself in the midst of my darkness... and they sent me to you. Thank you from the bottom of my heart!!!" ~ M.D., NC

"White Dove Circle of Light and Love has been life changing for me! I have personally been working with Heather to heal from past traumatic experiences and my life has changed since meeting her. Heather is wonderful and so SO gifted. She has helped me to release trauma and baggage that I have been storing for a long time. My physical health and mental health has improved so much since working with her. I feel lighter and less burdened and "stuck." The relationships in my life have improved as a result of her helping me to release certain things and untether myself from old wounds. She is a wonderful, kindhearted person who is truly gifted at what she does. I've also noticed a strong sense of community at White Dove Circle of Light and Love. They are genuinely focused on helping people and they do a wonderful job at it. I would highly recommend anyone looking for healing to visit. You certainly will not regret it!" ~ L.W., Dayton, OH

"I love going to White Dove Circle of Light and Love. Everyone is so welcoming and helpful. They are truly concerned about well-being. They offer a variety of services. My kids and I love the salt cave. My daughter & I love the amethyst biomat as well. The gift shop is large and stocks a huge assortment of gift items, healing items, etc." ~ A.SJ., OH

"I was telling someone about White Dove Circle and how it has changed my life over the last few years. I got carried away and spent almost 2 hours talking about all you do there!" - D.H., TN

"White Dove Wellness Center is a very welcoming respite from this sometimes crazy world! Pat Zimmerman, the founder and owner, has helped me stand upright without a cane through energy work, counseling, writing forgiveness letters to those who have hurt us, classes and her unwavering friendship. Spending 50 minutes in the Salt Cave is like escaping all your concerns & cares. I noticed the sinuses cleared, aches and pains were relieved. No pills needed! To say the least I love White Dove!" ~ Anonymous

"I started coming to White Dove Circle after a history of 8-12 seizures a day for about two years. After going to many hospitals and doctors for help, having had 6 brain operations and taking numerous pharmaceutical medications, nothing worked until finding White Dove Circle. The seizures disappeared practically overnight after coming to White Dove Circle. It's been several years since I have had a seizure. They are non-existent. My life has changed drastically for the better. Energy healing is the only way to heal!" ~ B.R., Springfield, OH

"This is a feedback for an amazing Healer and you may think of her as a truly intuitive kind of 'Therapy for the soul and body.' "If you are looking for an answer to any negative pattern in your life--stress, anxiety, help with teenagers or just to expand your spiritual and emotional positive journey, visit White Dove Circle in Springboro, Ohio and ask for Heather Bauer-Nilsen or other astonishing people that provide services that can fix or alleviate the root cause of health and soul peace and balance. "Thankful for your services and Heather's help." ~ CYV, OH

Amethyst Bed / Crystal Bed

"I had touched base with Pat to let her know I had broken my heel and was waiting on a surgery date. In conversation she had mentioned coming to WDC to try out the Amethyst mat she had just got in. Since I couldn't do Reiki on myself due to my break and not wanting the Reiki to heal the break without everything in place, I figured I had nothing to lose and it might help reduce the swelling so surgery could be done sooner rather than later! I mentioned bringing my husband down also as he had broke a rib 4 weeks prior and of course there is nothing that can be done for a broken rib! After 4 weeks he was still experiencing discomfort, pressure, and pain. Yes, together we were a hot mess!

"When we got there, I had my husband go first and then I went next and we compared notes. The mat was like a full body heating pad with amethyst rods that went the whole length on both sides of the mat. We each had a 30-minute session where we rested on the heated mat on our back fully clothed on the massage table. We both noticed that at first our pain in the area we were both having issues with intensified for a short period of time and then was completely gone. I noticed an excessive amount of heat in the area of my foot even though the heat in the pad was consistent throughout indicating that like Reiki, the energy was going to the area that needed the healing the most! When I got up from the table and put the air cast boot back on my foot fit the boot so much better as if the swelling had gone down. I no longer was feeling discomfort and several days later I had my doctor's appointment, and he was able to schedule the surgery because the swelling had gone down enough for him to operate.

"My husband walked out of WDC that day with no pain or discomfort and has not had any pain or discomfort since which was approximately 2 weeks ago! I highly recommend trying this healing modality out if you are in any pain or have chronic pain. We will definitely keep this in mind if we have any other issues. I look back on all the times our kids could have benefited from a session if it had been available. I am thankful it is available now at WDC!" ~ J.H., New Breman, OH

"I severely sprained my knee when I was out walking. After three weeks of being unable to bend my knee, walking with a limp, wearing a knee brace, and suffering through severe pain, I had come to the conclusion that maybe it was more than a sprain, and was considering seeing a doctor and possibly undergoing knee surgery. Then I had the opportunity to experience the Amethyst BioMat offered at The White Dove. In less than 24 hours the pain was completely gone. I had full range of motion in my knee. I was able to bend, squat, walk up and down the stairs, all with absolutely NO PAIN!! I put the knee brace away! This BioMat is the real deal! What a blessing to be able to avoid the doctor and possible surgery! I highly recommend the Amethyst BioMat for any kind of pain and any level of pain being experienced." S.R., Miamisburg, OH

White Dove Energy Blankets

Last month when we received the devastating news that Maddox was going to lose his right eye unless a miracle happened, I felt led to google "healing blanket" and found a website called whitedovecircle.com that makes healing blankets and infuses them with loving, healing energy from God's angels. I've been using the blanket with Maddox all month; and the wonderful people from the White Dove Circle organization have been lifting Maddox up in prayer with us also. I'd also like to point out that the day after I received the blanket in the mail, my Mom said she heard a voice telling her "What you need to heal Maddox is in the red box." She told me about the message she had received, even though she had absolutely no clue what it meant. I instantly thought of the red box that the blanket was mailed in. (My mom had no clue about the blanket or the box at that time). So, I'm feeling pretty thankful to have been led to this amazing group of people, and to have the powerful healing energy from the blankets they make surrounding my son! If you or anyone you know is in need of any type of healing (physical, emotional or spiritual), you should contact Patricia Zimmerman through the whitedovecircle.com website. These blankets are magical! *smile emoticon*

[Maddox was diagnosed with eye cancer on 8/5/11. Dr's said he would be blind forever, but we had total faith in his healing. Maddox now SEES everything!] – Miracles for Maddox (FaceBook page), V.B., VA

"My life has really improved in so many ways since I've had my healing blankets. I have four of my own and use them every day. They are kept in different rooms of the house so that they are easily accessible to me. The first healing blanket I got was from the first few that had the healing energy put in them, so it has been around for several years and it still works so well. They all have been washed many times and still have the same incredible healing power. You only need to use one at a time because they have such extra special soothing energy. They have been used to heal my wrist and elbow problems, back issues, ankle and feet issues. There have been times when I could hardly walk because of severe aches with my knees. When I go to bed, I wrap these around whatever part of my body is hurting and I wake up so refreshed in the morning. In fact, I never travel without a part of one of the special blankets. I used scissors and cut off about a twelve inch by five foot strip from the end of one of my blankets and it easily fits into my luggage, which is so nice for when I am flying and can't take many bags with me. I can't say enough about these miraculous blankets and how they and the White Dove Circle of Light and Love have changed my life." My life has really improved in so many ways since I've had my healing blankets. I have four of my own and use them every day. They are kept in different rooms of the house so that they are easily accessible to me." – D.G., New Lebanon, OH

"I have to say I love the healing blanket! Not only is it super soft, but it works! I was raking grass in our yard Saturday and was feeling sore all over. While watching a movie that evening, I cuddled up in my blanket. When we got up to go to bed, I felt great, no soreness, and I felt energized!" – L.G., IN

"After another church group sent me a "healing blanket" which was the size of an oversized placemat in colors which actually sent me for my prescription meds. I was genuinely skeptical of your online offer for help with your healing blanket. It arrived late today. I laundered it. Then took my necklace pendant off and with my husband, a retired engineer as witness, used my pendant as a pendulum…like magic it began moving in ever widening circles (!). I am a disabled RN. Fearing I was to the point in my pain control experience…four failure meds at the Pain Clinic…finally one with breakthrough pain meds and muscle relaxants...you name it…Neurontin to jump scar tissue synapses in the back muscles. Rev. Zimmerman, I will take my "vitamin" every day. Thank you for making it affordable. I hurt all over…even with Pain Clinic meds which keep me out of the ER with extreme pain. The doctor treating me said he is only "obliged" to cover 40$ of my pain. Perhaps God is intervening to cover the remaining 60%. Thank you for sharing your gift. Thank you for caring." – L.S., Detroit, MI

"I had the best night of sleep last night in months thanks to this blanket!! I'm so excited that my Healing blanket from White Dove Circle of Light and Love finally arrived. I had been planning on using it for my Reiki table, but it seems Nova and I need it more right now. Nova definitely senses the energy in the blanket too. I threw it on Tim's shoulders, and he said "Ooh it tingles!" (He can feel energy like that too when it's super strong) I'll have to get another for my Reiki table I highly recommend them. I was also very excited to get a restock of the balm I use on everything, especially my face. I slathered it on before work and someone asked what I was doing with my skin because it looked great. I'm almost 45! I've been using this cream for about 3 years. It is assisting my genetics for sure." ~D.L., NJ

"No doubt the best product you can buy uniquely at White Dove- everyone in my family has one…even our dog (don't forget how much our pets absorb our emotions to protect us). Everyone can benefit from having a healing blanket. Grateful for you and my friends at "The Dove" Pat!" ~ B.G., Cincinnati, OH

White Dove Hand & Body Balm

"Several years ago I had a major surgery that required a graft be taken from the underside of my forearm. Once the bandage was removed, I started applying White Dove Hand & Body Balm around and on the scar and graft area. I have been told by many doctors that they've never seen a graft that healed as nicely as mine. I believe using White Dove Hand & Body Balm attributed to that." ~ R.B., Covington, OH

"Recently I was heating a bowl of soup in my microwave. As I removed it the hot bowl tipped. The boiling soup spilled all over the top of my hand, the stove below and the cabinet where I set it down. I immediately ran it under cold water to reduce the temperature. It was bright red and very painful. I put White Dove Circle's Hand and Body Balm on it. The heat immediately melted the balm, and I kept applying it. It worked like a miracle. The red color left my hand, and it never blistered. Within an hour there was only a 2" area on one finger that had a burned area. In a week the old skin peeled off and you would never know that it had been burned. I had been told that the balm was good for burns, but I did not expect it to heal a burn of this depth so quickly. I use it for dry skin and other problems but never would have expected such a fast recovery from a burn that would have disabled me without the use of my right hand for quite a while. Although tender, I used my hand all day. I truly recommend that you have some of this around for emergencies. It works miracles!" ~ B.M., Naperville, IL

"Having a bad cold, I needed a lip moisturizer. I used Burt's Bees, but didn't see the Mango Butter ingredient and I'm allergic to Mango! Instant allergic reaction with a rash! White Dove Circle Hand and Body Balm healed it in 2 days!! Love this product! Patricia Zimmerman, this

is amazing! Love you, and love what you do for mankind!"
♡♡♡♡♡♡♡♡ - L.G., Estero, FL

"I was stung by a wasp today moving some bricks. I react very badly to wasp stings. In the few minutes it took me to go inside, the burning and swelling was the size of a blueberry. I washed my hand and applied your healing cream on the sting area. Within a few seconds the healing cream had turned to a liquid form, a minute later the stinging and burning was gone and 10 minutes later the swelling was gone. I can still see where I was stung but have no pain or swelling. I am so grateful to have your healing cream, it works better than anything I have ever tried. Thank you, I love you." – L.G., IN

"Works on age spots, too. Plus joint pain. Not to mention wrinkles. I use it on sore feet, bruises & dry skin. Heck, I use it on everything! Love it. Smells wonderful." – SLC, Brookville, OH

"Tonight, while getting my mail from the mailbox, I was stung twice by a yellow jacket. My arm turned red and began to swell. I used your balm on the stings and the pain went away immediately. I am so happy I have it on hand. Just wanted to say thank you. I appreciate your healing offerings." ~ A.B., Hanover, PA

BIBLIOGRAPHY

Jackson, Elliott Eli. *Sapiential Discourses: Universal Wisdom, Book III*. Amazon. 2017.

Jones, Aurelia Louise. *The Seven Sacred Flames*. Mt. Shasta, CA: Mt. Shasta Light Publishing, 2007.

Zimmerman, Patricia. *Self-Empowerment: The Only Way to Heal*. Dayton, OH: WDC Publishing Co., Inc., 2015.

Books Written by Patricia Zimmerman

- *Self-Empowerment: The Only Way to Heal* (2015)
- *Everyday Life Lessons: Living Life with Ease and Grace* (2018)
- *Everyday Life Lessons: Living Life with Ease and Grace, Companion Guide* (2018)
- *Boosting Your Immune System Nature's Way* (2020)
- *Releasing Cancer Nature's Way: True Healing and How to Achieve It* (2024)

Books Written by Robert and Charles Burton

- *Briellie's Tummy Ache* by Robert and Charles Burton (2021)

Made in the USA
Monee, IL
30 September 2024

66224421R00128